THE INTERNET FOR SENIORS MADE EASY

Find What You've Been Searching For

By James Bernstein

Contents

Introduction

With everything being "connected" these days, we tend to rely on the internet more and more just to get by with the basics such as paying bills, buying movie tickets, and communicating with friends and family. And if you are not online in one way or another, you might find yourself not being able to do things such as signing up for a cable or cell phone plan or finding an instruction manual for your new TV.

Keep in mind that if you prefer to do things the old-fashioned way (while you still can) that is fine, but it's always a good idea to get yourself acquainted with current ways of doing things for when the time comes where it's the only way to do them. Even if you can still do things like go to the local branch for your banking, buy your movie tickets in person, and call your friends on the phone, it doesn't mean it's not a good idea to start making the transition to the online world, even if it's just for simple web browsing purposes.

The goal of this book is to first get you acquainted with what the Internet is and how it works. Then I will focus on how you can use the Internet to make your life easier and more productive... and even more fun! I will also go over how to keep yourself safe from all of those bad people out there that are looking to take advantage of those who are not so tech savvy.

This book is not meant to be an advanced book on computing and the complex networking that makes all of the Internet magic happen but rather was, put together to give those who may not be the most technical people a leg up on how to increase their online skills and take advantage of all the things the Internet has to offer.

So, on that note, grab some coffee and your computer (or other device), and let's see what's out there and what all those millions of other people all over the world are doing!

Chapter 1 – What is the Internet?

When you hear the word *Internet*, what do you think of? Do you think of things like Google, Amazon, and Facebook, or do you think of it as a way to check your email, read the news and pay your bills? Regardless of what you think of, it's most likely that there is much more you can do on the Internet than you think.

Web browsing is just a part of what you can do with the Internet (even though I will be focusing a lot on this part of it since that's most likely what you will be doing on the Internet yourself). However, since it's such a big part of using the Internet, there are things you should know to make the most of it while keeping you and your personal information safe at the same time.

How the Internet Works
The Internet is a very complicated network of computers and other hardware which I won't be getting into too much detail about, but you might want to know the basics of how it all works just to satisfy any curiosity you might have.

The Internet is basically a network of computers (or servers) around the world that are all connected together using connections that are capable of communicating with each other to allow information to pass back and forth through these connections. Back in the beginning these connections were simple, but now they are very complex, and information has to travel through many paths to get where it's going. Just think about if you were visiting a website in another country or continent how far the text and images from that website have to travel to make it to your computer screen and how fast they get there. It's not like there is a single cable connecting your computer to the web server in that country, but rather multiple connections are being made to accomplish that task. Figure 1.1 shows the basic idea of your computer at home in the United States connecting to a web server in

Europe, and also to one in South America going to two different websites. It's not as simple as the one line between the two shown in the diagram makes it out to be, but rather multiple connections in many locations transferring the data back and forth between the computers. Web server is a term for a computer that hosts a website or multiple websites.

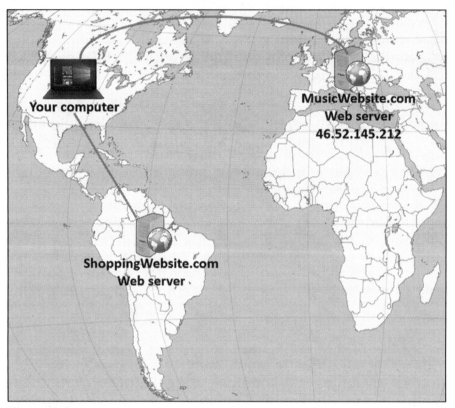

Figure 1.1

Your computer makes its connection to the web server by using the public address (IP address) of that web server. These public addresses are assigned to the companies that are hosting the web and are unique to that company. But rather than having to know the public IP address, which can look like 46.52.145.212, we use a service to translate the address of the web server into a friendly website name such as **google.com**. So, when you type the name of the website (such as ShoppingWebsite.com) into your web browser, this service knows that the address for ShoppingWebsite.com is 46.52.145.212 and sends you to the right place. Then the web server sends the data you requested (the web page) back to your computer, and you can now view it on your screen. Once that connection between your computer and the web server is made, it stays connected until it's broken when you do something like close your browser or disconnect from your wireless etc.

Ways to Connect to the Internet
In order to use the internet, you need to be able to connect to the internet. This can be done several ways and these ways may vary depending on what type of device you are trying to go online with such as a computer, smartphone or tablet etc.

If you are a smartphone user, then you will always have an internet connection since it uses the connection from your cell phone provider. You can also connect your smartphone to your Wi-Fi (wireless) connection at home to avoid using your cellular data plan and running out of data. Once you connect to your wireless, your phone will use that for the internet by default and once you are out of range of your wireless, it will automatically switch to your cellular connection which will most likely be a little slower.

 If you have an Android based smartphone and would like to know how to get the most out of it, then check out my book titled **Android Smartphones for Seniors Made Easy**.
https://www.amazon.com/dp/B0B14FW7JW

If you use a computer at home, then you can also connect to the internet via your wireless connection. You can also connect via a cable attached to your modem if your computer is close enough to it. If you do use your Wi-Fi connection, then it will connect the same way for any computer or phone you use to connect to it. You will need to know the name of your wireless connection and also the password. The process for making the connection will vary depending on what device you are using so if you need help getting online, you might have to ask a friend or family member.

Once you make your wireless connection, your device should remember the login information so next time you turn it on, it will connect automatically so you won't need to go through the process again. If you are connecting to your modem with a cable, you do not need to worry about entering a password to connect since it will do so automatically.

Things You Can Do Online
With the popularity of the internet constantly growing, you will find that there are more and more things you can do via the internet than ever before.

Of course, the most popular and commonly performed task is searching the internet which is also commonly referred to as browsing or surfing the internet. This is when you use a web browser and type in a search term and then view the various results of your search.

Sending and receiving emails is another popular thing to do online. This requires you to have an email account in order to send email to others and there are many free services that you can use such as Gmail, Outlook, Yahoo and AOL for example.

 If you would like to learn more about using email as well as the most popular email services, then check out my book titled **Email for Seniors Made Easy** https://www.amazon.com/dp/B09RV2KYTF

Many people like to use the internet to do their shopping since it's easy to find the best price by just visiting a few web pages rather than having to drive around to multiple stores. Then you can simply purchase the item right from the website and have it shipped directly to your house or pick it up at the store.

Paying bills and doing your banking is something you can do online to save yourself some time. Rather than having to write checks and mail them in, you can pay them right on the utility's website using your checking account or a credit card. And if you need to deposit a check or transfer money to a different account, you can do that online as well.

Many people like to play games on their phones and computers and it's possible to install games on your computer or even play the games that come with your computer such as solitaire. There are websites where you can play online games with other people or by yourself. You just need to make sure they are legitimate sites and don't let them install anything on your computer when you visit the website.

Watching videos online is a very popular thing to do since you can find videos on just about any subject. One of the most popular, if not the most popular video website is YouTube, and you can search for videos to watch and even upload your own.

Speaking of watching videos, there are also streaming sites such as Netflix and Hulu where you can watch movies and TV shows online and even on your smart TV if you have it connected to the internet. Most of these services will charge you a monthly fee to watch their content so be aware of that.

If you are the type who likes to keep in touch with friends and family, then you can use some of the many types of social media platforms to see what they are up to as well as share what you are doing. Some examples of these services include Facebook, Instagram, Twitter and so on.

 If you would like to learn more about how to use the most popular social medial platforms, then check out my book titled **Social Media for Seniors Made Easy.** https://www.amazon.com/dp/B09KN64W7M

Chapter 2 – Web Browsers and Search Engines

If you plan on using the Internet on a regular basis, then that will require you to use a web browser to do so because without one then you are not going to get too far… if anywhere at all. And if you are going to perform searches on the Internet, then you will need to use a search engine for that. One common mistake many people make is confusing a web browser with a search engine or thinking they are both the same thing when in fact they are not at all.

What's the Difference?

The difference between and web browser and a search engine comes down to that a web browser is software installed on your computer and is used to display web pages, while a search engine is a website that you use WITHIN a web browser to perform searches. So technically you are using a search engine website to search for other websites by using web browser software. Hopefully that doesn't sound like I am talking in circles!

After you read the next sections that go into details about web browsers and search engines, things will make a little more sense. Knowing the difference between the two will make you a more efficient web user and will also allow you to experiment with different web browsers and search engines to find the ones that work best for you. And yes, there is more than one of each!

Web Browsers

As I mentioned in the last section, web browsers are software installed on your computer that are used to display the content from websites such as Amazon or Facebook. Most computers should come with a web browser already installed, but you can install others and use more than one at a time. For example, Windows computers will come preinstalled with the Microsoft Edge web browser and Apple computers will come preinstalled with the Safari web browser. When reading this information, keep in mind that the process for various tasks will vary between browsers and it's impossible to show every process for every browser. Here is a listing of the more commonly used web browsers:

- Google Chrome
- Microsoft Edge
- Safari
- Mozilla Firefox
- Opera

As I mentioned before, you can install more than one web browser on your computer so you can try them out and find the one that you like best. For the most part, they all operate in a similar fashion, but they will vary in ways such as how the menu items are laid out, how bookmarks are used, and also how they perform. Plus they are all customizable to some degree so you can tweak them to your liking.

Figure 2.1 shows an example of the Microsoft Edge web browser that comes installed with Windows. As you can see, there are a lot of components that make up a web browser, but that doesn't mean you should be intimidated by them. You will also notice that the web browser has the Google search engine page opened within it.

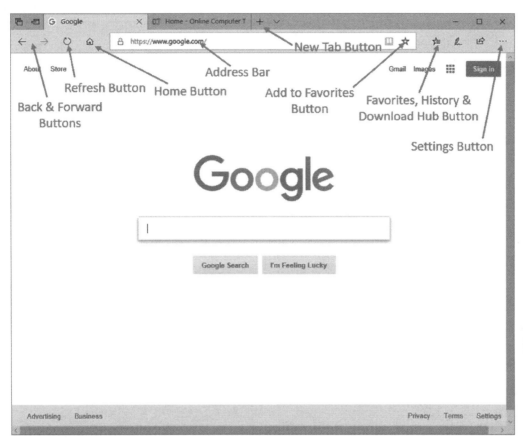

Figure 2.1

Now I will go over each of the main areas of a typical web browser. Keep in mind that they can vary a bit from browser to browser.

- **Address Bar** – This is where you type in the website addresses you want to go to if you prefer to do that rather than do a search for the site. (I will discuss addresses more later in the chapter.)

- **New Tab Button** – This will allow you to have multiple website pages open within your web browser. Simply click the new tab button which is usually a + sign and it will open up another page that you can use to browse to another site while leaving your other pages open. (I will go into tabs later in this chapter.)

- **Add to Favorites Button** – Use this button to add websites that you are on to your favorites so you can easily find them later and go back to them. Favorites are also known as bookmarks in other browsers.

- **Home Button** – Clicking on this button will take you to your home page, which can be customized to whatever you want it to be. Some browsers don't show the home button by default so keep that in mind if you don't see one on yours. You might need to get some assistance enabling it if you want to use it.

- **Refresh Button** – If you want to reload the web page you are on to check for updates or in case it doesn't seem to be responding, you can press this button.

- **Back & Forward Buttons** – You can cycle backward and forwards through all the pages you have been to within a certain tab with these buttons.

- **Favorites, History & Download** – If you go here, you can view your favorites or bookmarked sites, go through your browsing history, and also look at your downloaded files.

- **Settings Button** – This is where you can configure and customize your browser to suit your needs. You can also do things like set your default home page, clear your history, and check out your saved passwords.

 I like to stick with one web browser because once you start having it save things it will make things more complicated when switching back and forth between other browsers since one will most likely have information stored that another won't.

If you are up to the challenge and would like to try a different web browser you can simply go to the website for that browser, download the installation file, and install it like you would any other program on your computer.

Search Engines

Now that you have an idea of what a web browser is, I will now go over search engines. A search engine is a service that allows you to search for content on the Internet using your web browser. There are many companies that provide this service free of charge for you to use. The search engines go out on the internet and index its contents in their own databases so when you search for a specific word or phrase, it can find the websites that match what you are looking for.

You have most likely heard of Google, and they have the most popular search engine in use today. Providing search engines is not the only thing Google does, of course, but that is how they got their start and is one of the reasons they are such a huge company today. Here is a listing of some of the more popular search engines, and there are many more out there besides the ones in my list:

- Google
- Bing
- Yahoo
- Ask
- AOL
- DuckDuckGo

To get to a search engine all you need to do is type its address\URL (discussed later in the chapter) into the address bar of your browser. Or you can even use one search engine to do a search for a different search engine. For example, in figure 2.2 I used the Google search engine to do a search for Bing (the results are shown in figure 2.3). (I will get into more details about how to do web searches in Chapter 3.).

Q   bing   🎤

Figure 2.2

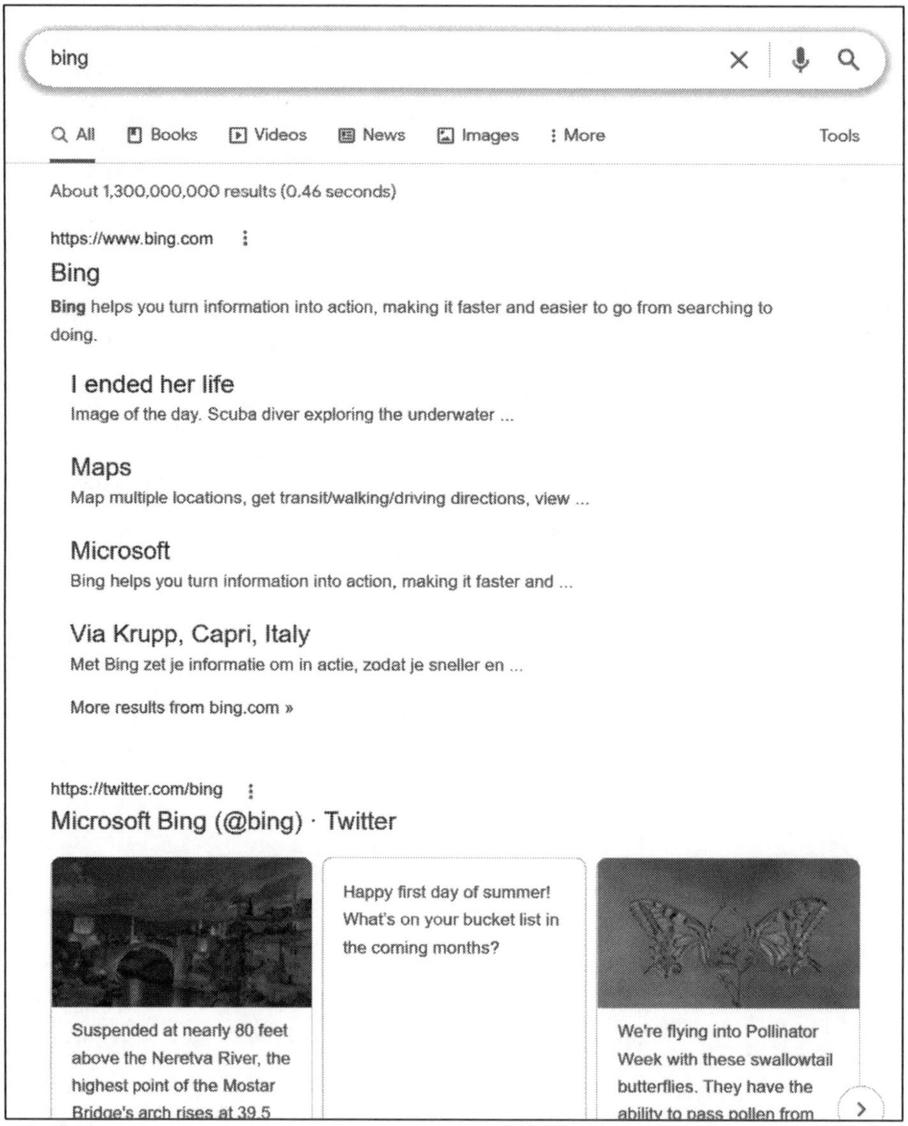

bing   ✕ | 🎤 | Q

Q All   📖 Books   ▶ Videos   📰 News   🖼 Images   ⋮ More   Tools

About 1,300,000,000 results (0.46 seconds)

https://www.bing.com   ⋮
Bing
Bing helps you turn information into action, making it faster and easier to go from searching to doing.

I ended her life
Image of the day. Scuba diver exploring the underwater ...

Maps
Map multiple locations, get transit/walking/driving directions, view ...

Microsoft
Bing helps you turn information into action, making it faster and ...

Via Krupp, Capri, Italy
Met Bing zet je informatie om in actie, zodat je sneller en ...

More results from bing.com »

https://twitter.com/bing   ⋮
Microsoft Bing (@bing) · Twitter

Happy first day of summer! What's on your bucket list in the coming months?

Suspended at nearly 80 feet above the Neretva River, the highest point of the Mostar Bridge's arch rises at 39.5

We're flying into Pollinator Week with these swallowtail butterflies. They have the ability to pass pollen from

Figure 2.3

Then when I click on the first result for Bing it will take me to www.bing.com, where I will then see something similar to figure 2.4. Then I can type in my search criteria in their search box and do my searches from there.

Figure 2.4

Using different search engines will yield different results for your searches since they are not all sharing the same information and build their databases and index the Internet differently from each other. So, if you are not getting the results you are looking for from one particular search engine, then you might want to try another. (I will go over how to perform effective searches in Chapter 3.)

Tabbed Browsing
One of the greatest inventions when it comes to web browsers is the addition of tabs which let you have more than one website open at a time. In the old days, if you wanted to be on two or more websites at a time, you would have to open multiple instances of your web browser. For those of us who have multiple websites open all day long, that can get messy, but thanks to tabbed browsing, things are a lot more organized and easier to get a handle on.

Figure 2.5 shows the Google Chrome web browser open with a single default tab. You will always have at least one tab open when using any web browser. Since my home page is set to google.com when I open my browser, it automatically goes to their website.

Figure 2.5

Next to that tab is a + sign, which is what I would click on to open up a new tab within my browser. Doing this does not close the existing tab, but rather opens up an additional one next to it (as seen in figure 2.6). Now I have the Google website open in the first tab, and *www.onlinecomputertips.com* open in the second tab, and I can go back and forth between them. By the way, most browsers will open your default home page when you click on a new tab.

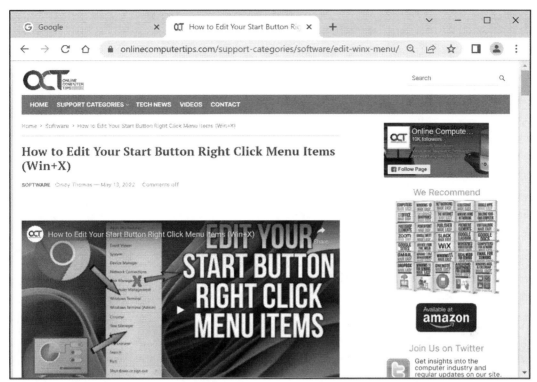

Figure 2.6

As you can see in figure 2.7, you can have as many tabs open as you want and switch back and forth between them. So, if you like to have your email, news, Facebook, YouTube, etc. pages all open at the same time, it's very easy to do.

Figure 2.7

If you don't like the order that your tabs are open, most browsers will let you drag them around to rearrange them however you see fit. And if you want to close a particular tab, simply click on the X on the tab itself and it will leave the others open. If you want to close all of them, then you can either do so one by one or simply close your web browser altogether.

 Many web browsers will allow you to configure them to remember what tabs you had open the next time you launch the browser. So, if you like to have the same 10 tabs open every time you re-open your browser, then you can do this fairly easily.

Bookmarks\Favorites

You will most likely find yourself having websites that they like to go to on a regular basis. But rather than have to remember what they are or what the website name is, they use bookmarks (or favorites as they are sometimes called) to save these websites in their web browser for easy access. Once you create a bookmark all you need to do is click on its name and it will take you to the exact website and page of that website that you were on when you created it.

These bookmarks are created and accessed differently depending on what web browser you are using, but the process is very similar between all of them. For example, figure 2.8 shows how to add the current page to your bookmarks by clicking on the three vertical dots at the top right of the browser window, and then choosing *Bookmarks* and the *Bookmark this page* option. In this example, I am using the Google Chrome web browser so how you do this in another browser such as Edge may vary a bit.

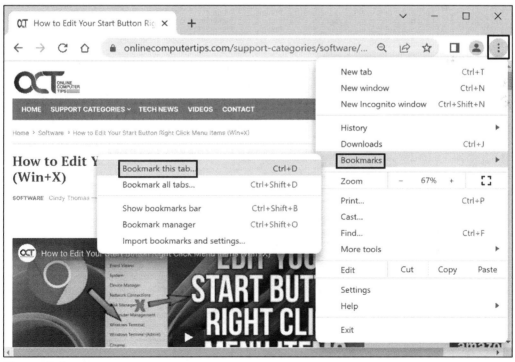

Figure 2.8

When you add a bookmark, you are prompted to give it a name or keep the name that it chooses, which is based on the webpage you are bookmarking. If you have bookmark folders, you can choose to have the bookmark placed in a specific folder.

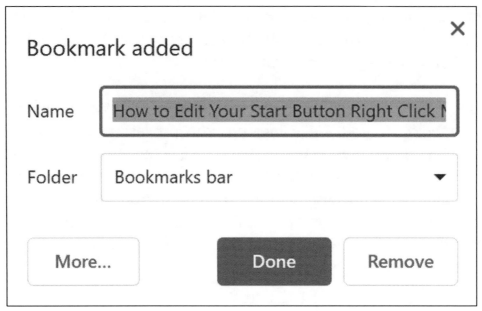

Figure 2.9

Figure 2.10 shows you how to add a favorite in Microsoft Edge by clicking the star icon to the right of the website's address at the top of the window. Remember that bookmarks and favorites are the same thing, and Microsoft is the one who usually refers to them as "favorites" while most other browsers use the term "bookmarks".

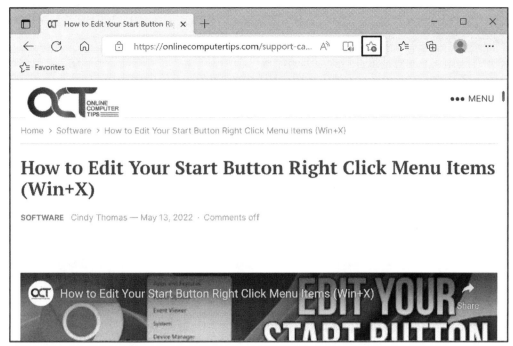

Figure 2.10

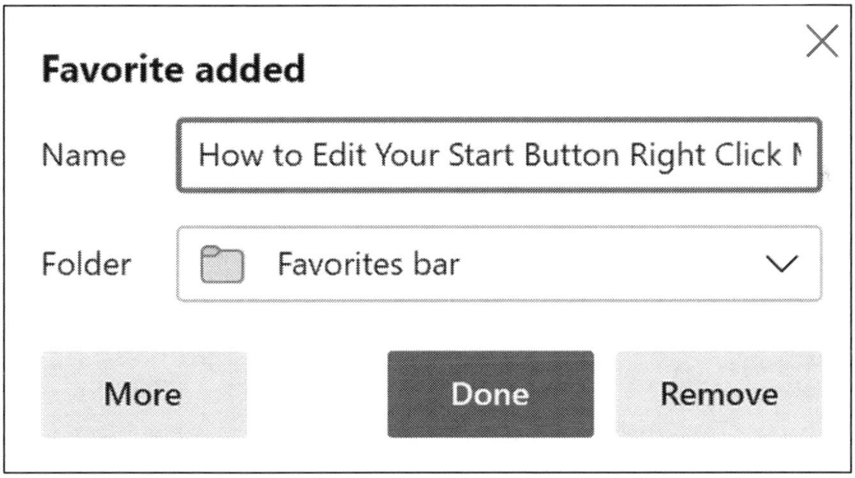

Figure 2.11

Most web browsers will also let you have a bookmark toolbar at the top of the browser where you can have your most commonly used bookmarks listed so you can simply click on the one you want without having to take the extra steps to go to your bookmark menu.

The process to access your bookmarks will vary depending on what browser you use, but all you really need to do is find where they are kept and click on the one you want to go to. Figure 2.12 shows how to access your bookmarks (favorites) using Microsoft Edge. It's also possible to edit your bookmarks to do things like rename them, delete them, and even change the address of where they point to.

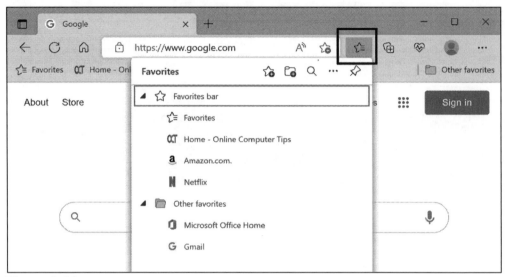

Figure 2.12

Website Addresses

All websites have addresses that are friendly names we use to connect to a web server located somewhere in the world. When you type in one of these friendly names into your web browser, your browser will translate it to the proper network address on the internet, so you are taken to the correct website.

You might have heard the term "domain name" being tossed around before, and that is the registered name used by that company on the internet. For example, the domain is microsoft.com, and anything after that is a part of that domain. You will even come across situations where there is something before the domain name such as **sales**.**microsoft.com**. So if you were thinking you were on the

Microsoft website, but something didn't look right, you could look at the address bar to make sure it had microsoft.com in the address. Figure 2.13 shows a valid Microsoft address while figure 2.14 shows an example of an address that doesn't look right and should alert you that you are not on the official Microsoft website.

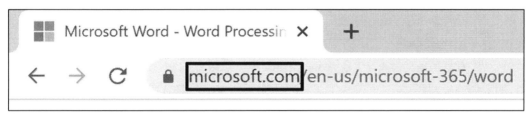

Figure 2.13

Figure 2.14

The main thing to remember about addresses is that if you know the address of the website, you can type it directly in the address bar rather than having to do a search for the website and find it in the search results.

Cookies

Everyone loves cookies right? Unfortunately, when you hear the word "cookies" when talking about web browsers and the Internet, it's not quite as delicious.

Cookies play an important part when it comes to your Internet activity and how your browsing experience goes. Cookies are small files that are placed on your computer by websites and are used by the website as a way for it to be able to recognize you and keep track of your preferences for that site. These cookies can either be temporary for the current visit to the site or permanent so they can be used the next time you go to that site.

These cookies can store various types of information and can be helpful, for the most part, even though there are many that can do things like track your web browsing history to be used for gathering information about you for advertising purposes, etc. For the most part, they store things like your name, email address, and other information so the next time you go to that website you don't need to enter it in again. One common thing that a cookie can do is keep track of the items you have in your cart while you are shopping online, so if you close your browser before checking out and open it again, the items will still be in your cart, and you don't have to start over.

It is possible to delete your cookies if you don't want them storing information about you and your online habits on your computer. Some third party cleaning programs will even let you delete just the cookies you want to get rid of while keeping others that you want to keep. To remove cookies from your web browser look for the section that lets you clear your browsing history and see if there is an option for cookies as well since not all browsers work the same way when it comes to cleanup. Figure 2.15 shows the *clear browsing data* dialog box from Google Chrome, and you can see how there is a section to remove the cookies from your computer. (I will be discussing browsing history and clearing saved data in Chapter 3.)

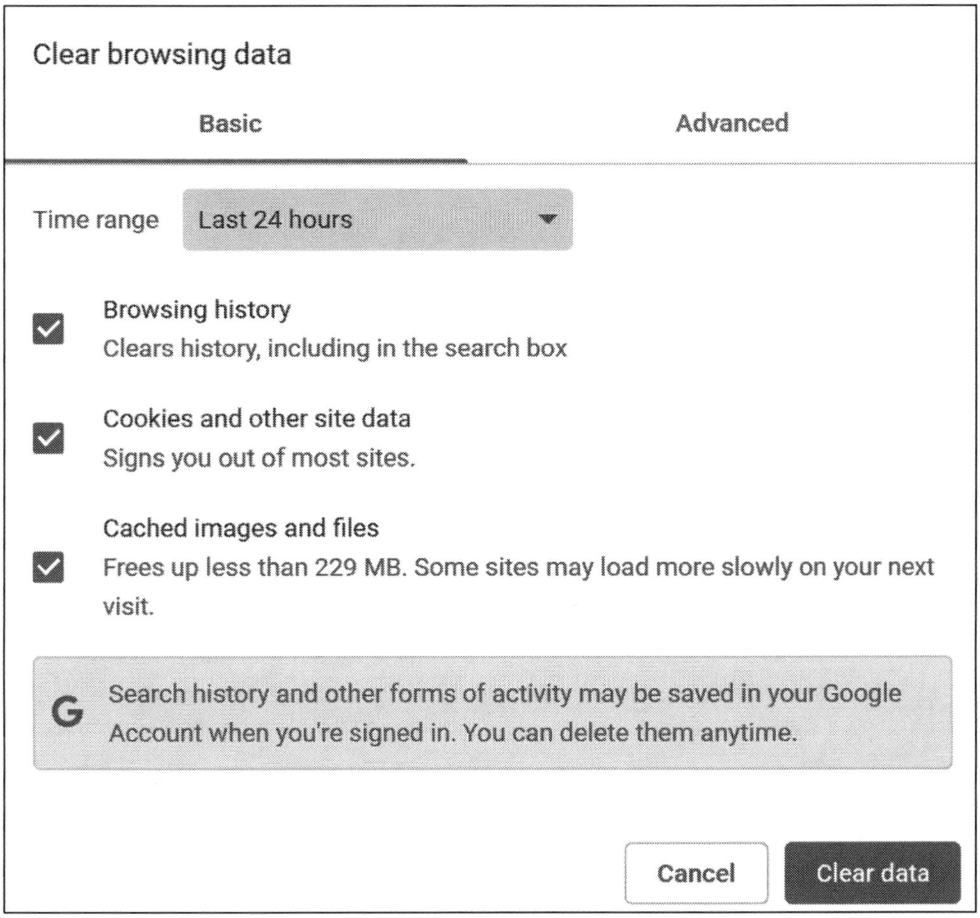

Clear browsing data

Basic	Advanced

Time range   Last 24 hours   ▼

☑ **Browsing history**
Clears history, including in the search box

☑ **Cookies and other site data**
Signs you out of most sites.

☑ **Cached images and files**
Frees up less than 229 MB. Some sites may load more slowly on your next visit.

G   Search history and other forms of activity may be saved in your Google Account when you're signed in. You can delete them anytime.

Cancel   **Clear data**

Figure 2.15

Many websites these days will ask you to accept their cookie policy and allow you to choose what types of cookies you will allow to be placed on your computer. Some websites won't even let you enter the site without accepting cookies so it's up to you.

Figure 2.16 shows a typical cookie popup, and you can see the cookie options where you can choose what types of cookies to accept and which to reject by sliding the selection button to the left or to the right.

Figure 2.16

I always choose just the necessary cookies and will uncheck any additional selections when presented with the option to choose. The less information people can get from you the better!

Storing Form Information and Passwords

The last thing I want to go over in this chapter is how you can save form information and passwords within your browser to make things easier and more convenient for you. But doing so may come at a cost!

Most, if not all, web browsers will let you store things such as addresses, passwords, and payment methods (credit cards) within the browser so you don't need to do things like type in your address on an order form, remember your password for a shopping site, or break out your wallet to make an online purchase. You may have noticed when signing up for an online account of some sort where you create a username and password that your browser might have asked you if you would like it to remember the new login information you created. If you say *yes*, then the next time you go to that website's login page the username and password will automatically be filled in for you.

Another thing you might have noticed is when you go to fill in an online form with your name and address that your browser will offer to complete it for you with the information it has stored from a previous form you have filled out. This can come in very handy if you are the type who doesn't like to type!

One downside to this convenience is the potential security risk involved. I will have an entire chapter on safety and security coming up, but for now I just wanted to mention that it's not a good idea to store login information and form information for certain sites such as banking websites in case your computer gets compromised.

Fortunately, if you have some stored information that you want to clear out, then you should be able to remove it from your web browser without too much effort but how you do this will vary depending on what web browser you are using so you may need to do a little research on your end or get some help from one of those computer geeks.

Chapter 3 – Surfing the Internet

Now that you have a better understating of how web browsers and search engines work and how they differ, it's time to start seeing what kind of interesting things we can find on the Internet. This chapter will be all about how to perform online searches and then how to decipher the results so you can find the information you are really looking for.

How to Effectively Search the Internet

There is more to searching the Internet than just putting in a word or phrase and pressing enter to see your results. Sure it will work fine for the most part, but there are other methods you can use to get more accurate results. On the other hand, if you can find what you need with simple searches then that's ok too, since most of the time that is what I do as well.

When typing in a word or phrase into a search engine, it will search for all of those words no matter what order you type them in. So if you type in **top rated dog food**, your results will be the same as if you typed in **dog rated food top,** as you can see in figures 3.1 and 3.2. The order of the results varies a bit, but it found the same information using either search term.

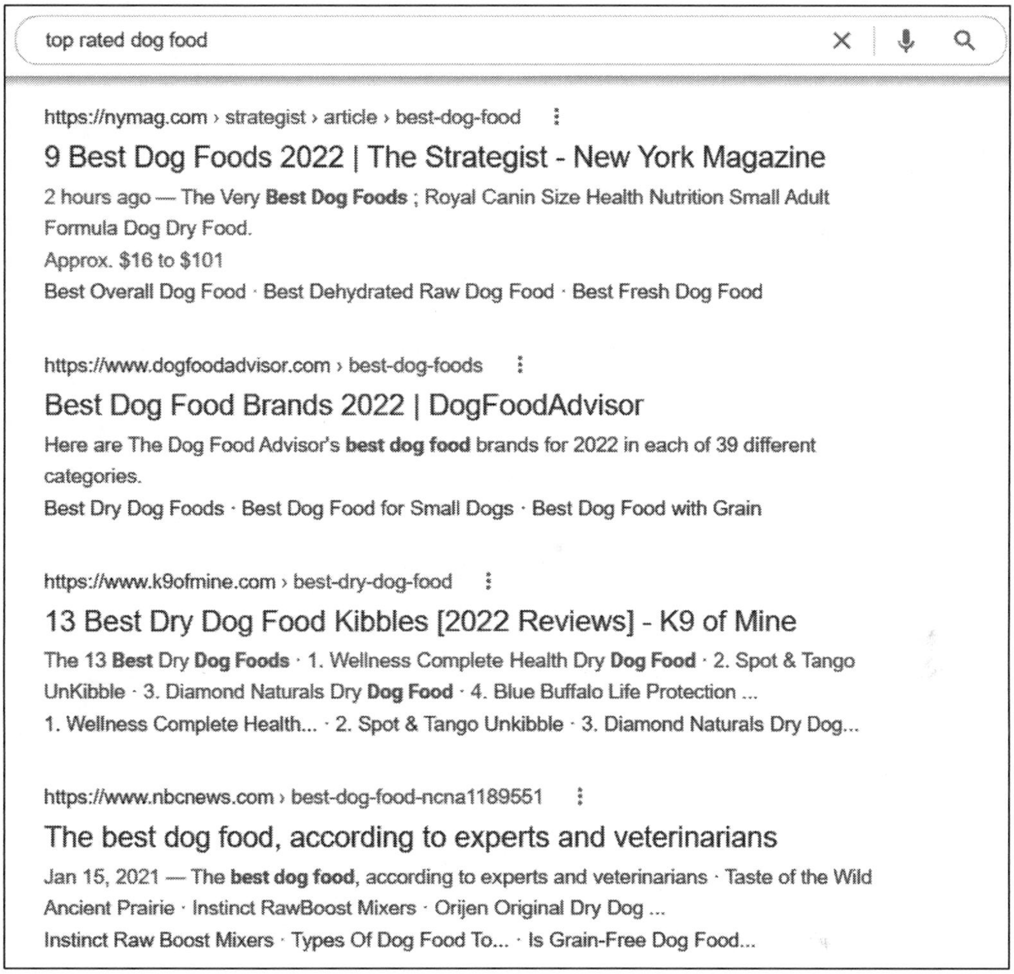

top rated dog food   ✕   🎤   🔍

---

https://nymag.com › strategist › article › best-dog-food ⋮

9 Best Dog Foods 2022 | The Strategist - New York Magazine

2 hours ago — The Very **Best Dog Foods** ; Royal Canin Size Health Nutrition Small Adult Formula Dog Dry Food.

Approx. $16 to $101

Best Overall Dog Food · Best Dehydrated Raw Dog Food · Best Fresh Dog Food

https://www.dogfoodadvisor.com › best-dog-foods ⋮

Best Dog Food Brands 2022 | DogFoodAdvisor

Here are The Dog Food Advisor's **best dog food** brands for 2022 in each of 39 different categories.

Best Dry Dog Foods · Best Dog Food for Small Dogs · Best Dog Food with Grain

https://www.k9ofmine.com › best-dry-dog-food ⋮

13 Best Dry Dog Food Kibbles [2022 Reviews] - K9 of Mine

The 13 **Best** Dry **Dog Foods** · 1. Wellness Complete Health Dry **Dog Food** · 2. Spot & Tango UnKibble · 3. Diamond Naturals Dry **Dog Food** · 4. Blue Buffalo Life Protection ...

1. Wellness Complete Health... · 2. Spot & Tango Unkibble · 3. Diamond Naturals Dry Dog...

https://www.nbcnews.com › best-dog-food-ncna1189551 ⋮

The best dog food, according to experts and veterinarians

Jan 15, 2021 — The **best dog food**, according to experts and veterinarians · Taste of the Wild Ancient Prairie · Instinct RawBoost Mixers · Orijen Original Dry Dog ...

Instinct Raw Boost Mixers · Types Of Dog Food To... · Is Grain-Free Dog Food...

Figure 3.1

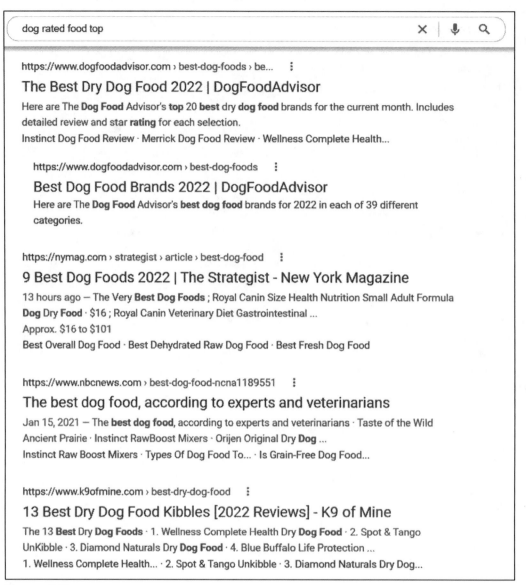

Figure 3.2

You want to be as specific as you can to avoid getting irrelevant results or too many results that you will have to sift through to find what you need. Many times you can even do your search in the form of a question, such as *what is the best computer for gaming* or *how do I make chicken alfredo* because it might be a commonly asked question or search term.

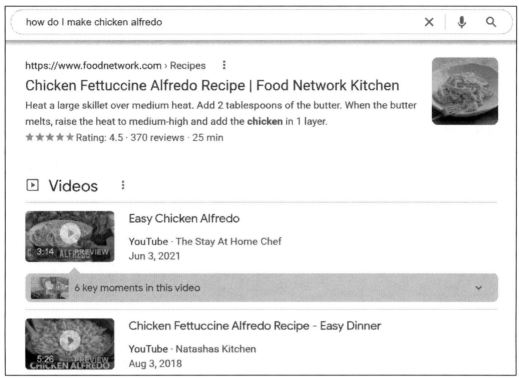

Figure 3.3

There are many tricks you can use to improve your search results, and I will now go over some of the more useful ones which you can then try out and see how they work for you.

Stay away from common words
Search engines will ignore most common words and characters such as "and" and "to", as well as certain single letters and digits because they tend to slow down your search without improving the search results. So try and design your searches to use more unique words that will give you less generic and unrelated results.

Use quotation marks for phrases
If you put quotes around your search phrase, then Google will find results that contain all of the words in the exact order you have entered them in the search box. For example, if you wanted to look up pages on Bill Gates but didn't want to get results containing other people named Bill or results about gates, you could type in "Bill Gates"

and you will get results with that exact phrase in it. You do not need to worry about capitalization either. You can also use this for longer phrases such as "blue 1963 Corvette convertible" if you wanted to get specific. Notice in figure 3.4 how Google found images matching blue 1963 Corvette, and in figure 3.5 found the exact phrase, which is highlighted in bold within the search results which can be seen by scrolling further down the page.

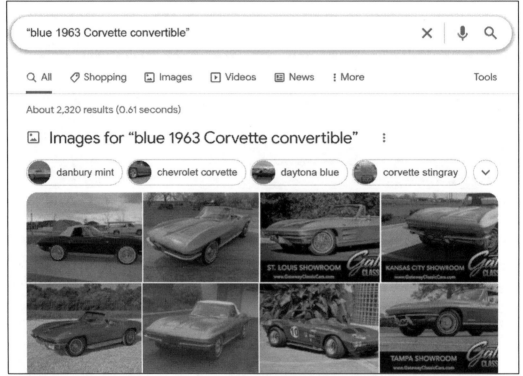

Figure 3.4

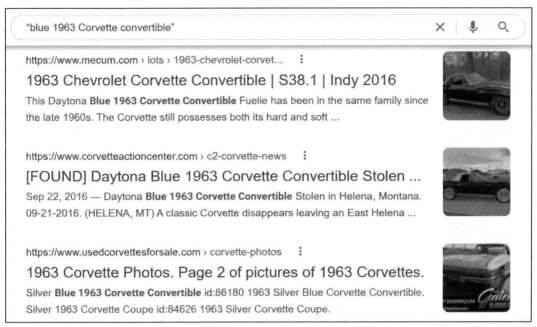

Figure 3.5

Using the "+" search variable
If you are looking for a certain thing on the Internet but need to include a specific word in your search results, then you can use the plus sign to have your browser include your keyword in its results. For example, if you were looking up TVs and wanted to include the Samsung brand in your search, you can type in **TV + Samsung** in the search box. Just make sure you put a space before the +.

*Using **OR** to find two results*
To find pages that include either of two search terms, add an uppercase **OR** between the terms. For example, if you wanted information about Princeton or Harvard University, you could search by **university Princeton OR Harvard**. Just make sure you use an uppercase OR.

These are just a few examples of how you can fine tune your searches. There are many other more advanced ways to perform searches so feel free to "search" for these methods online and try some out!

Sorting Through Search Results

Searching the Internet is one thing but trying to figure out what the results of your searches mean is a whole other issue. For the most part, search engines do a pretty good job of getting you the most accurate results based on your search terms, but they can still be a little confusing. Plus, with the abundance of advertisements being placed everywhere online, you will need to know the difference between a useful result and something that is just trying to get your money.

The results you get will vary depending on what search engine you are using. You may or may not also be presented with other results from your search related to things like shopping or images. For example, figures 3.6 and 3.7 shows a Google search result for the phrase **brown leather couch** with 106,000,000 results.

Figure 3.6 shows the top part of the search results which include advertisements about couches and figure 3.7 shows actual website results related to the search term a little further down the page.

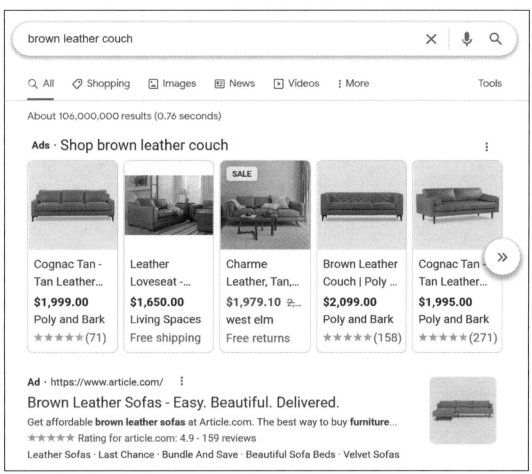

Figure 3.6

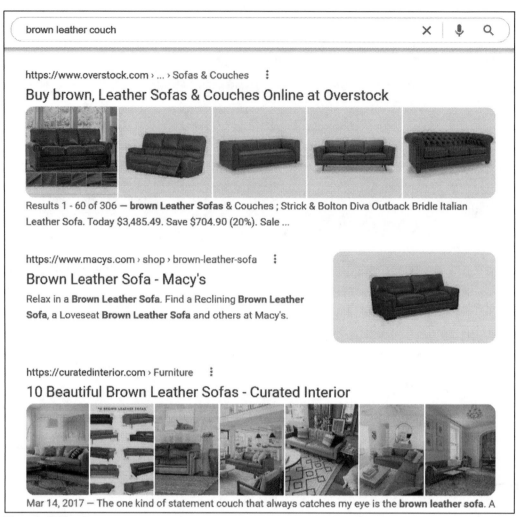

Figure 3.7

The results you get will vary depending on what search engine you use. So if I were to do the same search using Bing or Yahoo, I would get similar yet different results, and the advertisements and other results such as photos would be displayed differently.

Speaking of photos, when you perform a web search, you can have your search engine website show you different types of results based on your search term. Figure 3.8 shows the options offered by the Google search engine.

> brown leather couch
>
> Q All   Shopping   Images   News   Videos   : More
>
> About 106,000,000 results (0.76 seconds)

Figure 3.8

If you were to click on *Shopping*, you would be shown online stores that sell items related to your search term. If you were to click on *Images*, you would see pictures related to your search term as seen in figure 3.9. You could then click on any of the images to be taken to the website that the image is part of to get more information or see a larger photo.

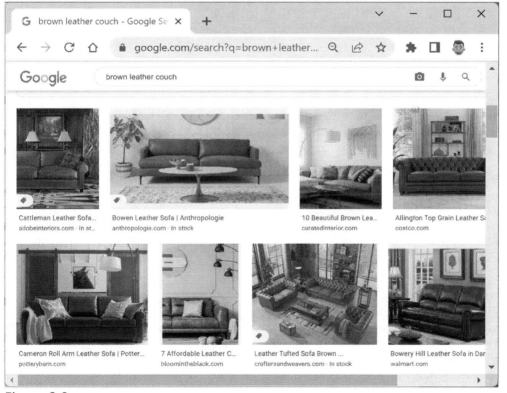

Figure 3.9

Going back to our search results, if you don't find what you are looking for on the first page, there will be many other pages you can sort through until you do. At the bottom of the search results will be page numbers that you can click on to go to the next page. Figure 3.10 shows some similar search terms you can click on if you feel they might get you better results, or you can simply go to the next page of the search results.

Figure 3.10

Figure 3.11 shows you the bottom of the search results page when using the Bing search engine. I just wanted to show you that things will look different depending on what web browser and search engine you are using.

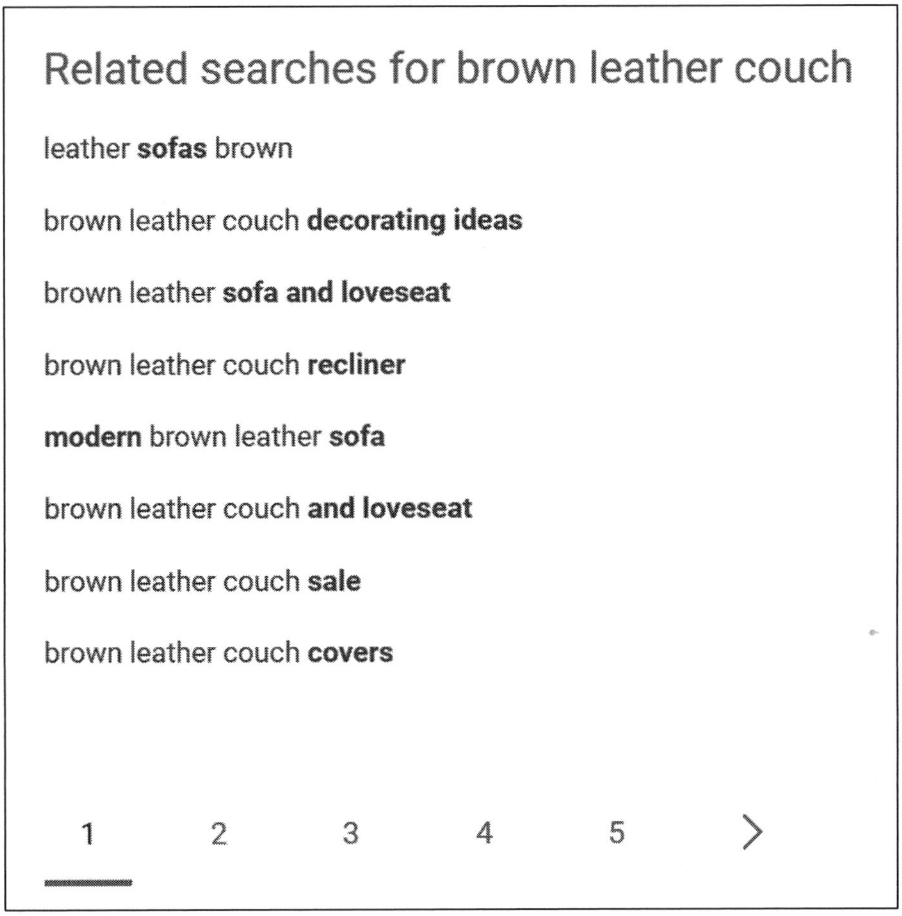

Related searches for brown leather couch

leather **sofas** brown

brown leather couch **decorating ideas**

brown leather **sofa and loveseat**

brown leather couch **recliner**

modern brown leather **sofa**

brown leather couch **and loveseat**

brown leather couch **sale**

brown leather couch **covers**

1   2   3   4   5   >

Figure 3.11

Once you find a result that looks like it might be of interest, you can simply click on the link to take you to that website. Figure 3.12 shows one of the results from my search. At the top you see the website address (macys.com) and then below that, you see the title and a description of the website page you would be going to if you were to click on the link. You might have also noticed that the search term (brown leather **sofa**) is highlighted in the results even though I searched for brown leather **couch**. Search engines know to use similar words such as automobile for car and blouse for shirt when displaying results for your searches.

https://www.macys.com › shop › brown-leather-sofa   ⋮

Brown Leather Sofa - Macy's

Relax in a **Brown Leather Sofa**. Find a Reclining **Brown Leather Sofa**, a Loveseat **Brown Leather Sofa** and others at Macy's.

Figure 3.12

If you don't like what you see, you can simply click the back button in your browser and go back to the search results and choose another one.

Saving Pictures and Text From Websites
When searching for things on the Internet, you might find that you want to save a particular image or paragraph of text to maybe show someone later or copy into an email to share with someone.

If you are doing a search specifically searching for a photo, then I suggest that you use the images feature of whatever search engine you are using for the best results like you saw for my couch search. Once you find the image, you want to make sure that you are saving the best quality version and not just a smaller thumbnail version.

For example, if you look at figure 3.13, you will see a bunch of Australian Shepherd dog images, and let's say you want to save the first one. If you did save it, then it would be a lower quality\smaller image than you would get if you clicked on it to have it show full size (like in figure 3.14).

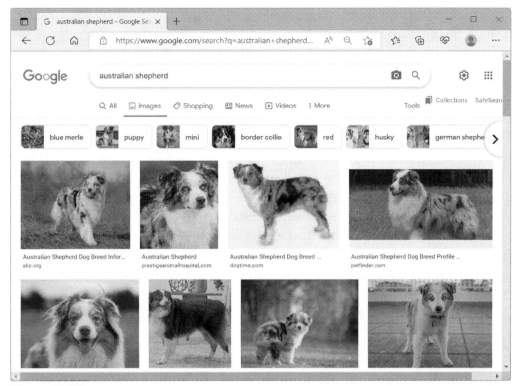

Figure 3.13

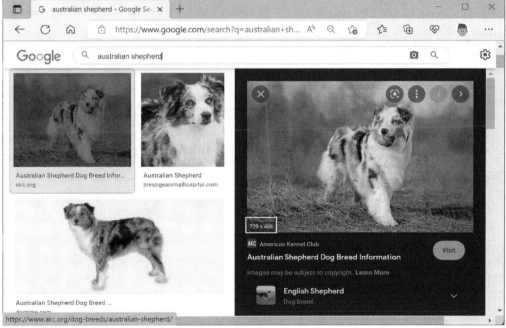

Figure 3.14

If you look closely at the bottom left corner of the image, you can see how it says 729 x 468 below the image. That is the size of the image in pixels, and the larger the numbers, the bigger the image will be, and most likely the better the quality.

If you want to see the image full size, you can right click on it and choose *Open image in new tab*, and it will show the image by itself at its real size. As I mentioned earlier, how things are done and the terminology used will vary based on what web browser and search engine you are using.

Figure 3.15

Now that I have the image full size, it's time to save it to the hard drive on my computer so I can use it later. To do so, right click anywhere on the picture and choose *Save image as* (or save picture as) and select a location on your computer that you will remember and be able to find later. You can also stick with the default file name, or type in anything you wish. Many people just save images to their desktop or pictures folder.

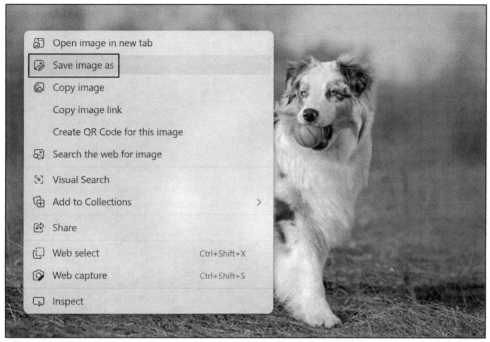

Figure 3.16

If you ever find an image that doesn't have any save options when you right click on it, that is most likely because they have disabled the saving feature for that web page.

When it comes to saving or copying text from a website, it is a bit easier process than saving pictures, and if you can copy and paste text from a document or email, then you shouldn't have any problem with this procedure.

Let's say I am on a particular website and found some useful information that I want to include in a document I am creating on Australian Shepherds. I have found the website I want to get the information from and have located the text that I want to save. So all

I need to do is use my mouse to highlight the text (as shown in figure 3.17), then right click anywhere on the highlighted text and choose Copy. (I can also use the Ctrl-C keyboard shortcut for Windows users, or Command-C for Mac users.)

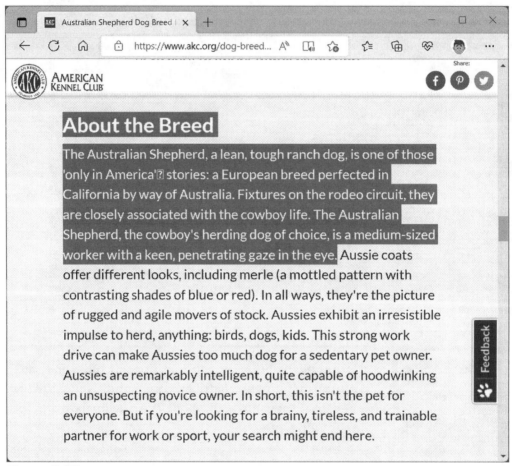

Figure 3.17

One issue you might run into is that when you paste the text into wherever you may want to place it, it will most likely keep the text formatting of the web page and not match up with the rest of your document (as you can see in figure 3.18). If this happens, then you will have to highlight the text that you just pasted in and change the font and formatting to match your other text. Or you can use the paste as plain text option from the program you are pasting the text into.

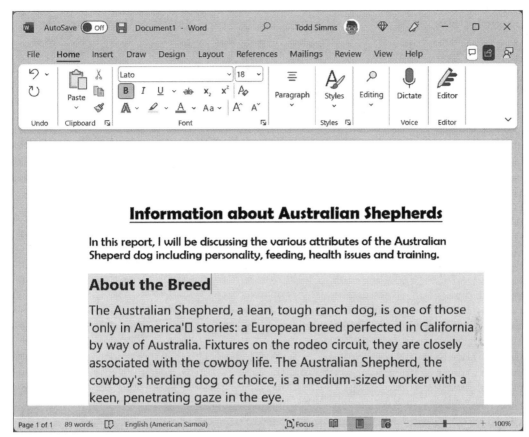

Figure 3.18

Browser History

After using your web browser of choice and going to many upon many websites, you may have the need to go back to a certain website but might not remember what it was called or its address. This is where browser history comes into play. Browser history is just like it sounds, an area in your web browser where you can go back and see what websites you have visited in the past.

Depending on what web browser you are using, your browsing history can be kept for time periods such as 90 days, 6 months, or even longer. You can even customize how long you want your history to be kept if desired.

How you view your history will depend on what browser you are using but is usually pretty easy to find in all of them. For example, figure 3.19 shows the history for Microsoft Edge, which can be accessed by clicking on the ellipsis at the upper right hand corner of the browser and choosing *History*. Then you will see all of your history sorted by date and time (figure 3.20). If you want to visit a site from your history, you can simply click on the site name itself and you will be taken back to the page linked to that history item.

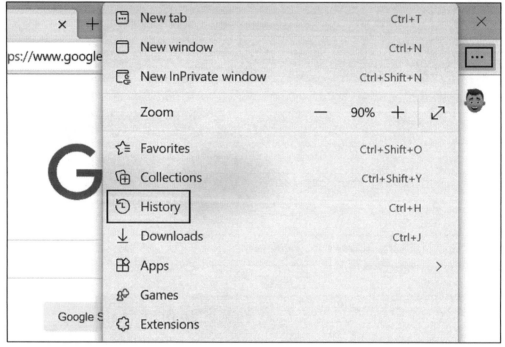

Figure 3.19

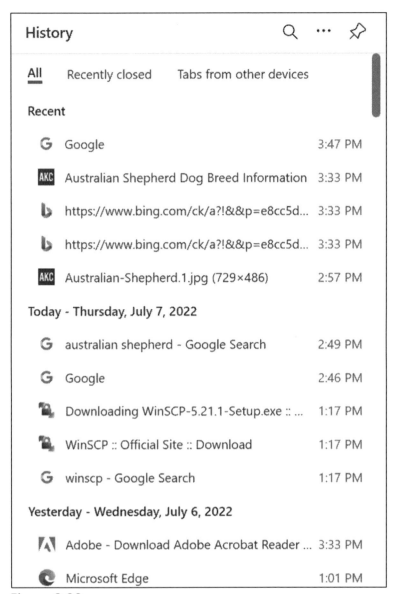

Figure 3.20

Sharing Websites with Other People

There will be many times when you are browsing the Internet and come across a website that you want to share with other people, and fortunately this is a very easy thing to do and there are a few ways to do so.

The easiest way to share a website is to copy the site's address and then paste it into something like an email or instant message chat box. If you know how to copy and paste text from something like a document, then this will be a piece of cake for you. Or if you read the section in this chapter about saving text from a website, then the same steps apply here, but the only difference will be what you are copying and pasting.

To copy a website address, what you need to do is click inside the address bar of your browser while on the page you want to share to have it highlight the address. Then you can right click anywhere on the highlighted area and choose *Copy* from the menu (as seen in figure 3.21). You can also use the shortcut keys that I went over earlier in this chapter.

Figure 3.21

Then you will need to open up your email or the messaging program that you want to use to share the website address, paste it in there, and send it to the person or people you want to share it with. They can then click on the link from that email or message and be taken to that exact same web page.

Most browsers will have a sharing option as well that will allow you to share a web page in more than one way. Figure 3.22 shows the Microsoft Edge *Share* option you can get to when clicking on the ellipsis like you did earlier to view your history.

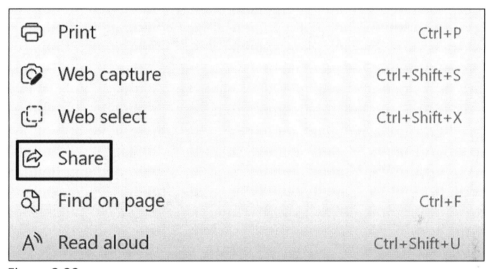

Figure 3.22

After you click on this option, you will have several methods to share the page (figure 3.23). The choices you see will vary depending on what apps you have installed on your computer and the sharing process used by other browsers such as Google Chrome will vary as well.

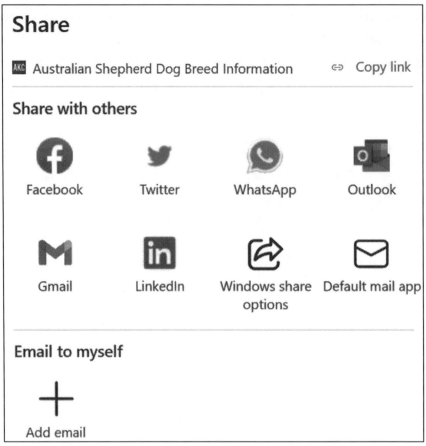

Figure 3.23

Online Games

The Internet is not just about doing research and paying bills but is also for having fun and killing (or wasting) time. And what better way to kill some time than with video games? You may think that you need to buy or install games on your computer in order to play them. And even though those types of games tend to be better in regard to how they look and what they can do, that doesn't mean you need to install any to have some fun.

The type of online games I want to discuss doesn't involve purchasing or installing any software to play and are played via your web browser. One thing I want to stress is **if you find a free online game and it wants you to download and install something to play it, then you should**

say no and get off that website because it's most likely going to install some type of spyware on your computer that will be used to do things like track your web surfing or steal your personal information.

Since I'm not a "gamer" I can't tell you which gaming sites are the best, but you can do a search for something like online games or free online games and see what you come up with. As you can see in figure 3.24, I get a mere 3.5 billion results when I search for online games, so have fun searching through all of the results!

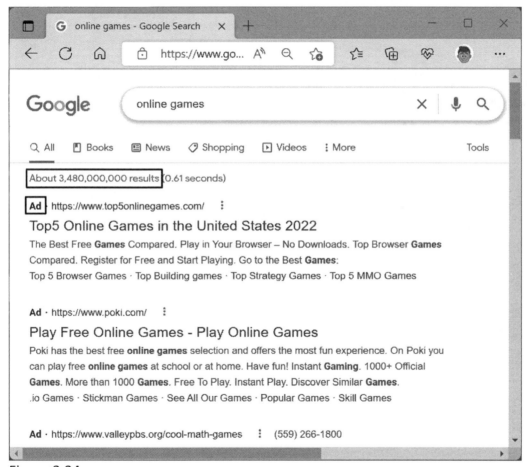

Figure 3.24

You can also see that the first 3 results are advertisements because they say **Ad** next to them. If I were to use Bing instead of Google to search, you can see I get a different result. I get 2.3 billion results and am shown a game called Microsoft Jewel that I can play right away.

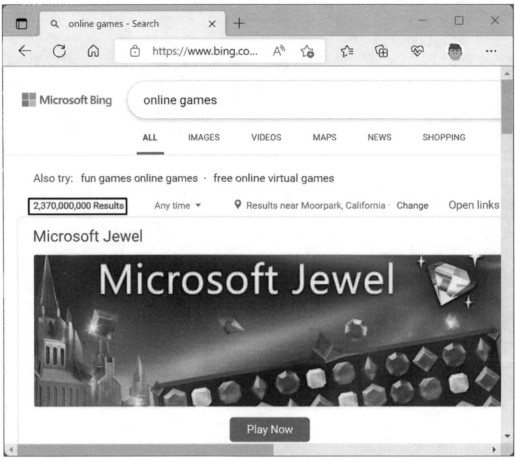

Figure 3.25

Going back to my Google results, I will scroll down the page and then click on the link that says *Free Games Online* with the website address of *www.arkadium.com*.

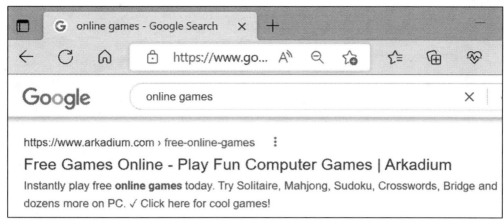

Figure 3.26

I am then shown several games that I can play, and I will click on the one that says *Free Online Classic Solitaire.*

Figure 3.27

After watching an advertisement video, I can now play the Solitaire game online from within my web browser.

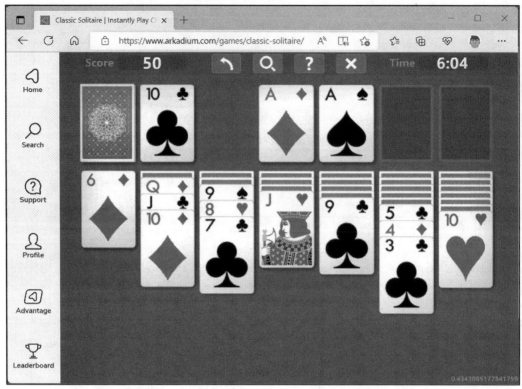

Figure 3.28

Speaking of ads, when playing these free games online, you will most likely be bombarded by ads and you need to be careful not to click on them, so you don't get taken to another website that you most likely don't want to go to.

TIP Your computer may have come with some games such as Solitaire preinstalled so if you want to avoid some hassle and play the games on your computer, you might want to do that instead of going online.

Chapter 4 – Online Email

Besides using the internet to perform searches, shop and play games, many people also use it to send and receive email with others to stay in touch. Email has been around almost as long as the internet itself and there are many email services you can use for free so you can communicate with friends and family. In this chapter, I will be going over the basics of how email works just in case you are new to using email yourself or maybe want to pick up some additional information on the topic.

Email Services & Software

Some of the more common email services include Gmail, Outlook (Hotmail), Yahoo Email and even the classic AOL which has been around since the beginning.

If you would like to learn more about using Gmail or how to use your email in general, then check out my books titled **Gmail Made Easy** and **Email for Seniors Made Easy**.
https://www.amazon.com/dp/B09PW3TRMX
https://www.amazon.com/dp/B09RV2KYTF

It's up to you to decide which email service you want to sign up for so you might want to see what services other people you know are using so you can have someone to help you out just in case you need it.

To sign up for a free email account, all you need to do is go to the website of the email service you wish to use. Then you will sign up for a new account and have to choose an email address that is not already taken by someone else. You will be informed if your choice has already been used and then you can try something else. Then you will need to come up with a password for your new account. Just be sure to make it at least a little complex with lower case letters, uppercase letters, numbers and special characters such as !@#$%^&*. An example of a reasonably complex password would look something like **Seahawks72#**.

After you get your account configured, you can simply sign in, and then you will be taken to your new email inbox where you can start sending out emails to whomever you wish. Just be sure you let the recipient know who you are the first time otherwise they may think it's junk mail!

Many years ago, it was common to have an email program (client) installed on your computer that would download your email to your computer, and then you could read it or reply to it using your software. One commonly used email client that is still very popular today is Microsoft Outlook. As a matter of fact, back when AOL first started, you needed to install their software on your computer to check your email.

These days, it's much more common to check your email on a website rather than on your computer. That way you don't need to have special software installed and can send email from your account using your web browser. Plus you can then use any computer, tablet, or smartphone to check your email as long as it's connected to the internet.

Figure 4.1 shows an email account using the Microsoft Outlook email client that is installed on the computer while figure 4.2 shows the same email account configured with the Outlook.com online email service. By the way, online email is commonly referred to as *webmail*.

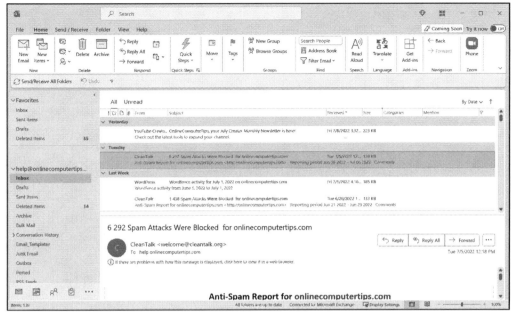

Figure 4.1

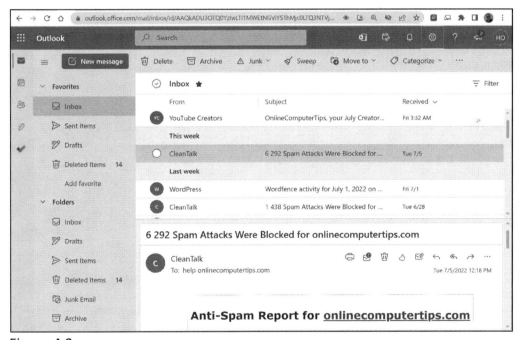

Figure 4.2

As you can see, the Outlook program and the Outlook webmail look similar in their layout with the folders on the left and the email in the middle. Most email clients and services will have a similar layout.

Sending and Receiving Email

For the most part, the process for sending and receiving email will be very similar no matter what email service you are using. Figure 4.3 shows how the new message box looks when sending an email from an Outlook.com email address.

As you can see, you have the *To* section where you will type in the email address of the person you want to send it to. If you have this person in your contact list, you can click on the To button to select them from your contacts and have them added to the email. This comes in handy so you don't have to remember their email address and can simply click on their contact's name to have them added.

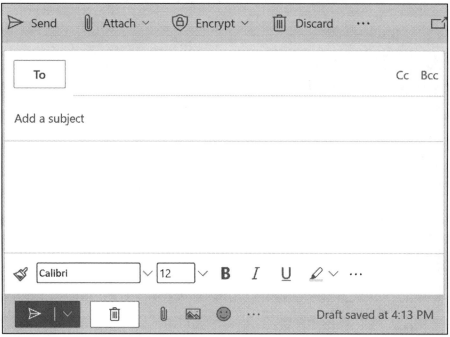

Figure 4.3

Below that, you have the subject line where you will type in the subject of the email. Try not to make the subject too long but rather keep any additional information for the main part of the email. Speaking of the main part of the email, below that is where you type in your actual message.

All email services will allow you to format your text as in change the font, make it larger or smaller, or do things such as make the text colored, bold or underlined. These formatting options can be seen at the bottom of figure 4.3 and figure 4.4. Figure 4.4 shows an example of an email that is being sent to two people and has the subject and message filled in and formatted.

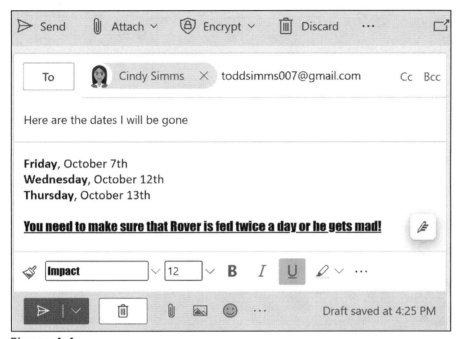

Figure 4.4

As you can see on the To line, Cindy is shown with her full name since she was in my contacts while the other person is shown with only their email address because they were not in my contact list.

If everything looks good, I can simply click on the *Send* button to have my message sent. If I change my mind, I can click on the trash can icon to delete it (before sending it). The bottom right corner shows me that there was a draft saved so if I don't send the message and close my browser, I could come back later and go to my *Drafts* folder to find the message and continue working on it. I will be working on this email later in the chapter so I can add some attachments and pictures.

When it comes to reading emails, it's simply a matter of opening them up and seeing what the sender has to say. Figure 4.5 shows a typical email inbox, and you can see several email messages on the right side. They are all bold except for the one from Microsoft and this means that I have not read any of them except for the Microsoft message. Once you read or open an email, it becomes marked as read and the bold attribute is removed. You can mark an email as not read even if you have read it if you want to have it appear as new again.

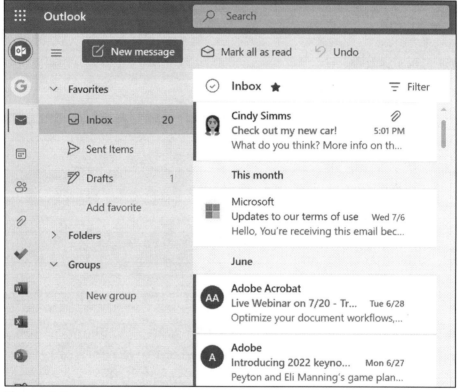

Figure 4.5

The email at the top is from Cindy Simms and she is sending me a message about her new car. If I open the email, I can see it more clearly as shown in figure 4.6. This particular email has a picture attachment of a car, and the email shows a preview of the attachment. This is different than having a picture be part of the email which can be done by pasting in a picture in the body of the email rather than attaching an actual image file itself.

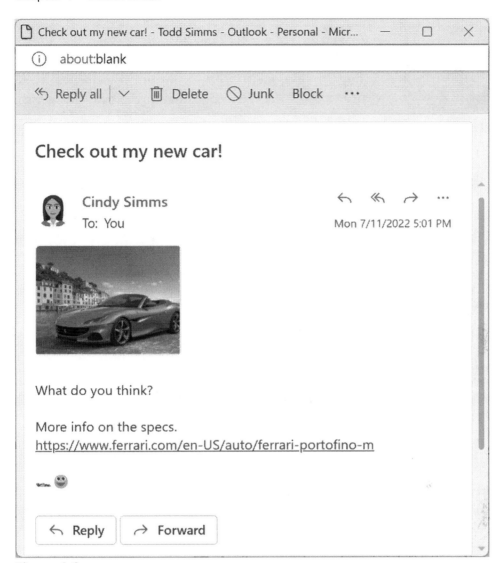

Figure 4.6

If I were to click on the car picture attachment, it would open up in a larger view and I would also have the option to download the picture to my computer. Other email services may or may not handle attachments in the same way. Then if I were to click on the link (underlined text), I would be taken to the website associated with that link.

 Be careful when clicking on links, especially from emails where you do not know the sender because they can take you to websites where you can get your information stolen or have malicious software installed on your computer.

At the bottom of the email you will see a *Forward* and *Reply* button. If I wanted to send this email to another person, I would click on forward and then enter their email address and then click on Send. If I wanted to reply to the sender of this email, I would click on Reply, type my response and then click on Send.

Attaching Pictures, Documents and Other Files

One commonly used feature of email is the ability to send files to other people so that can receive them within minutes rather than having to hand deliver them on a disk or flash drive for example. This comes in really handy if the person you are sending the file to is on the other side of the country, or in an entirely different country!

The process of attaching files to an email is fairly simple but you need to be aware of certain things when doing so. For example, there are size limits on attachments, and these vary between email services so you can't send the high definition video from your vacation in an email because it will be rejected because of its size.

Photos can also be an issue since today's cameras and smartphones take such high quality pictures which tend to make them larger in size when it comes to the file size itself. So if you need to send many pictures, you might be stuck breaking them up into multiple emails if you don't know how to reduce the size of your pictures first.

Other files such as documents tend to not be as large unless they contain a lot of images within them but even so, they are usually more manageable than photographs or videos. It's safe to assume that you will not be able to email video files unless they are very short or very low quality which will make the file size smaller.

To attach a file to an email you will need to compose a new message or reply to an existing message and look for the attachment icon which is usually represented by a paperclip.

Figure 4.7 shows a new email composed in Gmail with the attachment paperclip icon highlighted as well as the attached image file (Rover.jpg). The number *324K* next to the file tells you how large the attachment is and if you can learn how these numbers work, it will really help you determine if your attachments are too large or not.

Figure 4.7

When you click on the attachment icon, you will need to know how to browse the files and folders on your computer to find the file or files you are looking for. This is very important to know how to do if you want to be able to send attachments in your email. You can send more than one attachment at a time so if I want to attach an additional picture, all I need to do is click the paperclip icon again and choose my other file.

If I want to remove one or both of the attachments, I can just click on the X next to the name of the particular attachment.

Figure 4.8

Spam and Junk Email

Once you start using your email account for a time, you will start to see emails appear from people you don't know usually trying to get you to sign up for something or click a link to a website that you probably shouldn't go to. This type of email is referred to as junk mail or spam, and both terms are interchangeable.

The reason you get junk mail is if you ever sign up for something on a website and give them your email address, many times they will use it to send you email you don't want or even worse, sell your email address to others so they can use it to send you even more email that you don't want.

A lot of the time you can tell when an email is junk based on the subject and who it is from. If you don't recognize the name or email address and the subject is something like "check out this free TV offer," then you know it's not legitimate. There is a chapter at the end of the book on how to stay safe online so be sure to read that one carefully to avoid many of the internet scams that are out there.

Your email service should have a way to block or report spam to help you keep it to a minimum. If you receive an email that is spam, you should use the block or report option so your email service will not allow email from that sender to come to your inbox again. If it's not completely blocked, the spam might automatically send it to your junk mail folder, so you don't have to deal with it. To mark an email as junk or spam, you can check the box next to it and then click on the appropriate button depending on your email service. Figure 4.9 shows a few examples of where to find the spam or junk mail button with various email types (AOL, Outlook & Gmail).

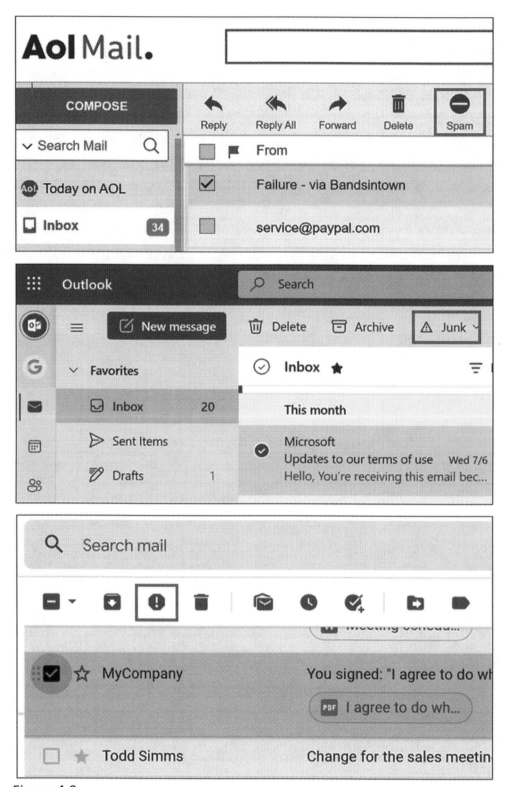

Figure 4.9

 When marking emails as spam or junk, it's better to do so from your main email list rather than opening the email first and then clicking the spam button. This is because hackers can create emails that can compromise your computer just by opening them.

Once you click the button to report the spam, it should be sent to your junk or spam folder where it will either stay or get automatically cleared out after a set amount of time depending on what you are using for your email account. Or it might simply be deleted altogether so you don't have to worry about it. You can also go into this folder and delete all of the junk mail manually if you choose.

As you start to mark email as junk, you will notice that you will see less and less of it because it will either be blocked or moved directly to your junk mail folder. If you do accidentally open one of these emails, just be sure not to click on any links or open any attachments because you might be asking for trouble! If you accidentally mark an email as junk, you can go into your junk folder and then mark it as not junk to avoid having it sent to that folder the next time you receive an email from that address.

Chapter 5 – Watching Videos Online

One of the most commonly performed activities that people do on the Internet is stream movies and music. With today's super-fast Internet speeds, it's easy to stream movies and TV shows in high quality HD format from the internet straight to your TV or computer.

There are many upon many ways to get your favorite movies, TV shows, and even music on your various devices, and trying to figure out what's best for you and your budget can get a little overwhelming. I would recommend using your newfound searching skills to see what's out there and find some real personal reviews to give you a better idea of what's best for you.

Video Streaming Services & Devices

I'm sure you have heard of services such as Netflix and Hulu for movies and TV and Pandora and Spotify for music, but there are many more services out there that offer similar content. You will need to decide if it's movies you are looking for or just certain TV shows and find out what providers offer what you need. It's unlikely that you will find one service that offers everything you are looking for, so you will either need to make some sacrifices, or get more than one service subscription.

Another thing to consider is if the service you choose is supported on all of your devices and that there is either no limit, or a reasonable limit on how many of your devices you can access your account from. For example, if you sign up for a movie streaming service and it will only allow you to register five of your devices (computers, tablets, smartphones, etc.) and you have six devices, then you will not be able to watch movies on one of them without removing one device from your account first.

You also need to make sure that all of the devices you want to use are supported by that streaming. So, for example, if you sign up for Netflix, you should make sure there is a Netflix app for your TV if you plan on using it on that particular TV. For the most part, all major streaming services will work on all types of devices.

Computers and mobile devices are pretty straightforward to get working with streaming services because you generally either just go to their website or launch their app to get yourself going. But if you want to use your TV, then that can be a little more complicated. TVs can also have apps that are used to access online content, and if you have what they call a smart TV, then you should be ready to go, assuming you connected it to your wireless Internet connection at home. If not, then you will need to find the settings section on the TV, look for wireless or networking settings, and connect to your Wi-Fi connection just like you would with a computer or tablet. If you don't have the app for your service, then there is a good chance you can search for it and install it on your TV. Most newer Blu-Ray or DVD players also have the capability to stream content as well if you don't have a smart TV, assuming you still use one of these.

There are also other specialty devices such as Roku adapters, Apple TV boxes, Amazon Fire boxes, and so on that you can attach to your TV and use to stream your content. They usually connect to an HDMI port on your TV just like your Blu-Ray player would.

Figure 5.1

Just to get your research started, here is a list of some of the more popular movie and TV streaming services. Some are free while others require a subscription.

- Netflix
- Amazon Prime Video
- HBO Go
- Hulu
- Sling
- Vevo
- Crackle
- Pluto TV
- YouTube TV

YouTube and Other Video Sites
YouTube can technically be called a streaming site, but it's not the same as the others that I mentioned earlier because the videos that are available for viewing on YouTube are made by other Internet users

such as yourself, and then uploaded to the site for others to watch. These videos can be as pointless as someone filming their cat sleeping, to something super informative such as a step-by-step tutorial on how to build a computer. Believe it or not, there are 300 hours of new videos uploaded to YouTube every minute!

YouTube does now have its own pay for streaming service called YouTube TV, and it offers content such as news, sports, and movie channels. Many of them are the same that you would get with your cable TV service, except you can watch these channels anywhere you have an Internet connection.

When you go to the YouTube website (www.youtube.com) you will see things like recommended and suggested videos that YouTube thinks you may like. These are based on previous videos you have watched if you have been there before. If not, then they will just suggest some trending videos for you to watch.

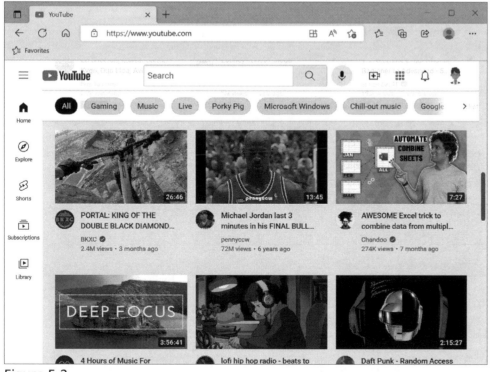

Figure 5.2

YouTube works the same way as a web browser where you type in a search for what you want to find. Figure 5.3 shows the results when I type in *funny dog videos* for my search.

You can then browse through the results and click on the ones you want to play. If you want to go back to the results, simply click the back button on your browser like you would for another website.

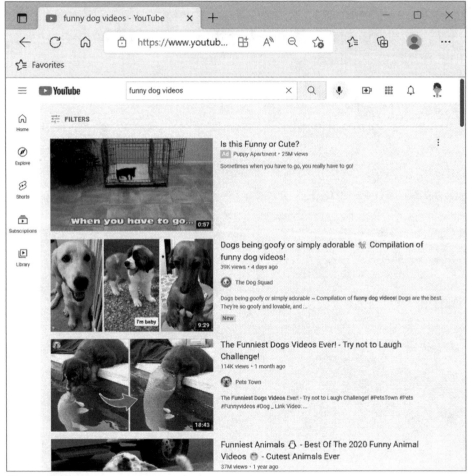

Figure 5.3

You can see various information about each video such as how many people have watched it, when it was posted and who posted it. In figure 5.4 you can see the video was posted only 4 days ago and already has 39,000 views. The user who posted the video is named The

Dog Squad and you can click on their name to be taken to their YouTube channel where you can see their other videos. At the bottom right of the video preview, you can see that this video is 9 minutes and 29 seconds in length.

Figure 5.4

When you click on a video to play it, you will be given suggestions for recommended videos based on what you are watching on the right that you can also watch. Just be careful not to get stuck watching videos all day, because it's really easy to do!

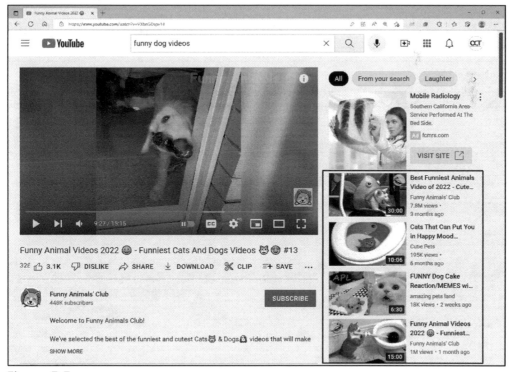

Figure 5.5

When you watch a video, you will notice several icons at the bottom of the video screen. Figure 5.6 shows you what each one does, and it should be pretty self-explanatory. If you want to fast forward a video, you can simply put your mouse cursor on the video time location bar and move it forward or backward.

Figure 5.6

Figure 5.7 shows what each of the sections below the video are used for.

Figure 5.7

For the most part, these should be easy to understand, but I will go over a few that might not be so straightforward.

- **Auto Play** – If enabled, the next video in the list will play automatically as soon as the current video is finished.

- **Closed captioning** – This is used to show text on the screen that matches what the person is saying in the video.

- **Quality** – Here you can change the quality of the video if you would like to see it in a higher resolution.

- **Sharing** – This option will let you do things such as share the video on social media sites like Facebook and Twitter and also allow you to share it via email and with other methods depending on what type of device you happen to be on at the moment.

- **Subscribe** – Clicking this button will add your YouTube account to that particular user's subscription list, and when they release new videos, you will be notified via email. If you are not logged into YouTube, then this action will not happen if you click the button.

- **Clip** – This is a newer feature used to send a particular part of the video to someone else so they can just view the part you would like them to see.

- **Save** – This option lets you save the video to a watch list that you can go back to later and view it when you want.

Chapter 6 - Online Shopping

One of the best parts of the Internet is the ability to shop for pretty much anything you will ever need all from the comfort of your chair, or even your couch. There are so many ways to buy so many different types of things from around the world, and once you find them, you can have them shipped right to your door, sometimes the next day... or even the same day!

Thanks to online shopping, you no longer need to drive from store to store to find what you are looking for. Even if you plan on getting your item from a local store, you can still shop for it on their website and even buy it online and then pick it up at the physical store the same day. Or, if you want to send someone a gift, then you can ship the item directly to their house instead of yours.

Many physical stores will even price match with deals you find online, so if you would rather get your item locally but pay the online price, then that is one way to go. (For the most part, this is usually available with larger retailers, and the online price needs to be from a reputable site.)

How Online Shopping Sites Work
There are many choices when it comes to buying products online and the process is pretty simple once you get used to it. Online shopping is similar to performing web searches because you simply type what you are looking for in the search box and then sift through the results with the main difference being the results will only be from one website (for the most part). Then once you find what you need, you select it and then make your purchase.

Amazon
The most popular shopping site of all at the moment is amazon.com, and they have been the most popular for many years now. You can find just about anything you need on Amazon, and have it shipped to

you in record time if you like. Since it's so popular, I will spend some time going over the site to show you how it works to get you used to the online shopping process and then apply what you learned to other shopping websites. Then if you decide to make an account for yourself or already have one, you will have a better idea of how to get around and make the most of your shopping experience.

Figure 6.1 shows the main Amazon website, and yours will not look exactly the same since the site changes constantly with new ads displayed and also products shown that are based on what Amazon thinks you may be interested in. One thing that will stay constant is the items on the top of that page that you use to navigate the site itself.

The first thing I want to point out at the upper left hand corner of the page is how in my example it says Amazon Prime. Prime is an additional service or subscription that you can sign up for that gives you benefits such as no minimum order for free shipping, free two day and even same day delivery, music streaming, free movies and TV shows, and so on. The cost of Prime is $139 per year or $14.99 per month. College students can get Prime Student for $59 per year (or $6.49 per month).

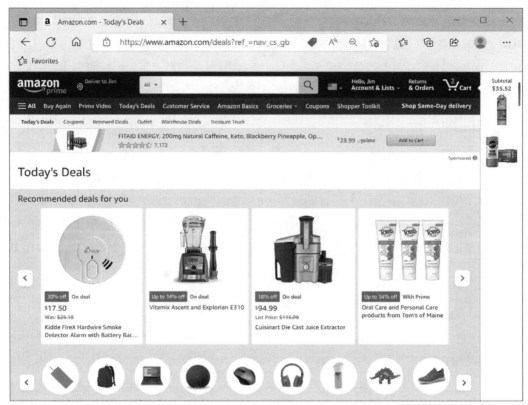

Figure 6.1

The Amazon site menu options can be accessed from the three horizontal bars in the upper left corner next to the word *All*. From there, you will have many items to choose from such as searching for videos and music, searching for particular products or departments, and browsing Amazon services. Take some time and go through the choices that sound interesting to you so you can get an idea of what you can do on the site.

Figure 6.2

The search bar works the same way it does when using a search engine like Google or Bing, but in this case, you can only find things that are available on the Amazon website. If you do a search for something like weather, you most likely won't get the results you are looking for! Figure 6.3 shows the results when searching for coffee machines. As you can see, you get the results in the main section of the page, and you will get many pages of results for an item as common as a coffee machine. Fortunately, you can sort by price, customer reviews, and newest arrivals from the Sort by drop down menu at the upper right corner of the window.

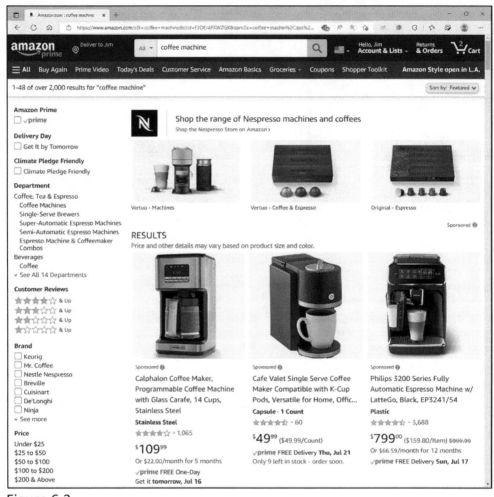

Figure 6.3

On the left hand side of the page you will have other options to help narrow down your search. If you are a Prime member, you can have it only show results that are Prime eligible. Or you can narrow it down by department or brand if the results are too vague. I like how you can also have it show results based on their average customer review, so if you want to see blenders that have a four star rating or higher, for example, you can do that by clicking on the four star review section under *Customer Reviews*.

Accounts and Lists at the top right of the window is where you can check your account settings and set preferences to enhance your shopping experience. For the most part, you won't do much here, but if you need to do things like change your shipping address or email address you would do so from here. It's also where you will go to add or edit payment information such as stored credit cards.

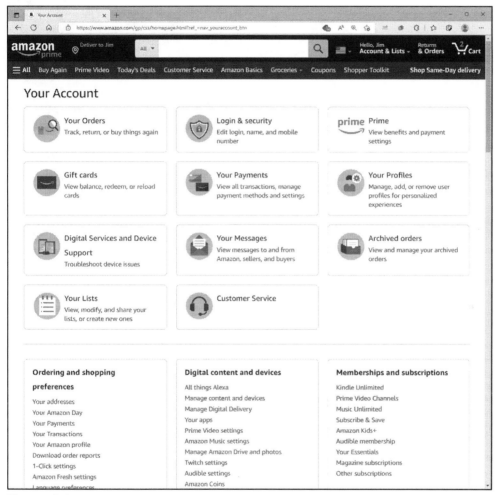

Figure 6.4

Amazon makes it really easy to track your orders and see what you have ordered in the past (which makes reordering items very easy). If you click on *Orders*, it will show you items that you have ordered that are in progress, as well as orders from the past that you have already received. Figure 6.5 shows that I have some items that were just delivered, and also shows that I have placed 76 orders in the past 3 months. I think I have a shopping problem!

If you look to the right of any one of the orders, you will see that you have many options to choose from. You can track the package if it hasn't been delivered yet, as well as start the return process if you need to send a product back that you don't like or was defective. Once you have purchased an item, you will be able to rate the product and write your own review for that item that others can read.

If you are looking for a particular item that you bought, then you can do a search for it using the *search all orders* box. This comes in handy if you want to reorder something again and want to make sure you get the exact same thing. Then you can click on the *Buy it again* button to reorder the item again.

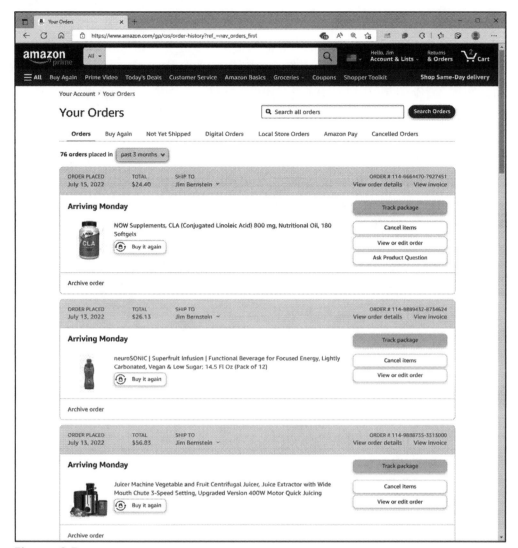

Figure 6.5

Figure 6.6 shows a product page for a coffee machine that I have clicked on. As you can see, you get the description, pictures, and customer reviews for this particular item. It will also tell you the delivery timeframe so you have an idea of when you will get it if you order it. For many items on Amazon you have the option to buy them used, but use your better judgment when doing so, especially on electronics and other things that can stop working. For many items, you can buy a protection plan to extend your warranty in case your item does decide to stop working on you.

There are two options when it comes to buying an item. If you click on *Add to Cart*, it will simply put that item in your virtual shopping cart, and you can check out later and actually make the purchase. If you click on *Buy Now*, it will automatically make the purchase for you using your default shipping address and payment method and bypass the shopping cart.

If you do add an item to your cart, it will show up in the top right in the shopping cart icon (figure 6.7). Then you can click on the cart icon itself to go to your actual shopping cart (figure 6.8).

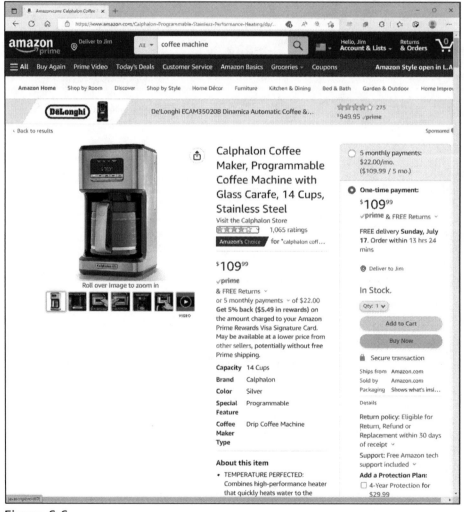

Figure 6.6

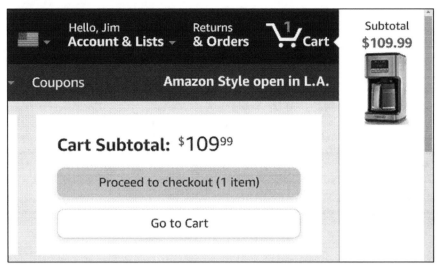

Figure 6.7

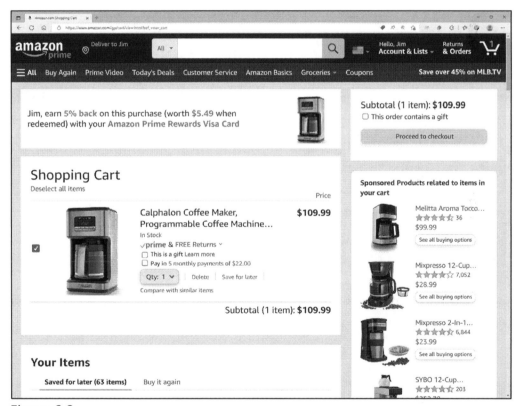

Figure 6.8

Take a look at the options underneath the item in the cart. As you can see, you can delete the item from your cart, save it for later, change the quantity, or compare it with other items. The *save it for later* option will just move it out of your cart and put it underneath so you can still have it around in case you want to move it back to your cart.

Figure 6.9

When you are ready to buy the items in your cart simply click on the *Proceed to checkout* button and you will see a screen similar to figure 6.10. Then you can confirm your shipping address, payment method, and the items and quantities to be shipped. If you have an Amazon gift card, you can enter the card number under *payment method* to have the gift card amount subtracted from your total.

Section 3 shows your delivery options. Since I have Prime, I can get it delivered to me as early as Sunday or pick a different date that works better for me. Many times you can get the item the next day or even the same day if you are a Prime member. Sometimes if you want an item faster you will have a choice to pay for expedited shipping if the faster shipping option is not available.

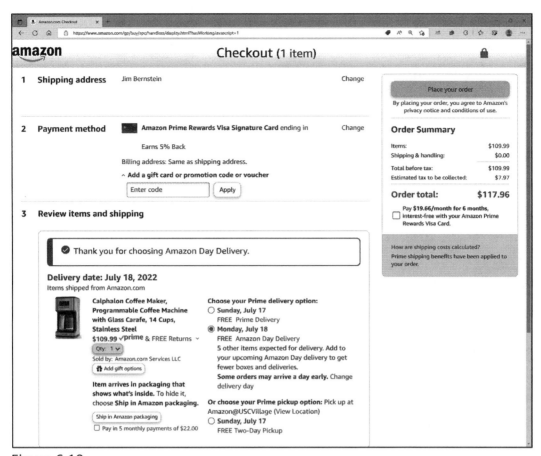

Figure 6.10

If everything looks good, then you can click on the *Place your order* button and then you will be given a confirmation screen that you can review for accuracy. You will also get an email confirmation as well.

Other Sites

There are many upon many other shopping sites online, and some are dedicated to specific products such as electronics or clothing while others offer products from just about any category. Rather than go through more examples from other sites that will look similar to the previous examples, I will just give you a listing of some of the more popular online shopping sites that you can check out for yourself. The shopping experience of these sites will be very similar to Amazon so if you can figure out how to use Amazon, the other sites should be a breeze.

- Etsy.com
- Target.com
- Walmart.com
- Wish.com
- BestBuy.com
- HomeDepot.com
- Ebay.com
- Overstock.com

Don't forget that you can also shop from your search engine search results like I briefly discussed earlier in this book. So, for example, if I were to search for *coffee makers* on Google, I would see the shopping results as seen in figure 6.11. The main difference will be that the results will be from various shopping sites around the globe and not just from one online retailer. If you look at the first result, you can see that under the item title it says from 10+ stores, meaning Google found that particular blender for sale from over 10 online retailers.

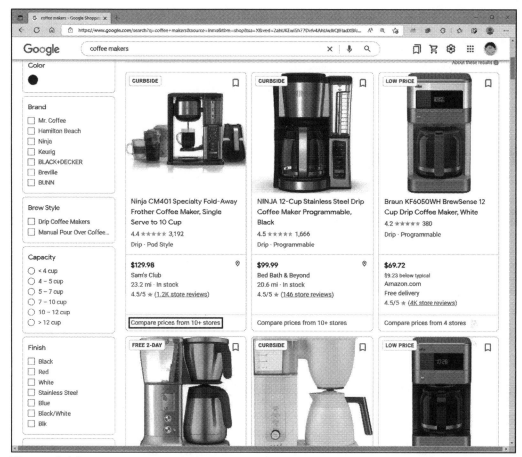

Figure 6.11

Product Reviews

When shopping online or even at your local store, it's nice to be able to find out what experiences other shoppers have had who have purchased the same product that you are interested in buying. Most sites will offer their customers the opportunity to post a review of the product they have bought so that other customers can hear their thoughts on things like the quality of the product, shipping time, and so on.

Product reviews are not what they used to be, and by that, I mean you can't trust them as much as you could in the old days. Many companies find ways to alter these overall ratings by doing things such as paying others to post fake reviews or using other mischievous methods. This doesn't mean all reviews are fake, but when you see a bunch of five star reviews along with a bunch of one star reviews, it makes you wonder how that product can have that many reviews on both sides of the scale. What I like to do is look at the three and four star reviews to hopefully get the most honest reviews. Of course, many of the five star reviews are valid as well, so it doesn't hurt to read those. I also find that many of the one star reviews are from people who just like to hear themselves complain or had a bad experience that was just a fluke or has nothing to do with the product itself (such as a box that was damaged during shipping).

For my review example, I will go back to Amazon, pick another coffee machine, and show you the reviews for it. Figure 6.12 shows that this blender has over 34,000 customer reviews, which is quite a lot of reviews in general. If you look at the stars, it shows that the average review rating for this blender is about 4.5 stars.

Figure 6.12

Clicking on the down arrow next to the stars will show you the percentage that each star has towards the total rating. If you look at figure 6.13, you will see that 70% of the reviewers gave it a five star rating.

Figure 6.13

Clicking on *See all customer reviews* will allow you to dig deeper into the reviews and sort or filter the results such as sorting by most recent or the top reviews (figure 6.14). If you want to see all of the one star reviews, for example, then you can click where it says 1 star and see only those results (figure 6.15).

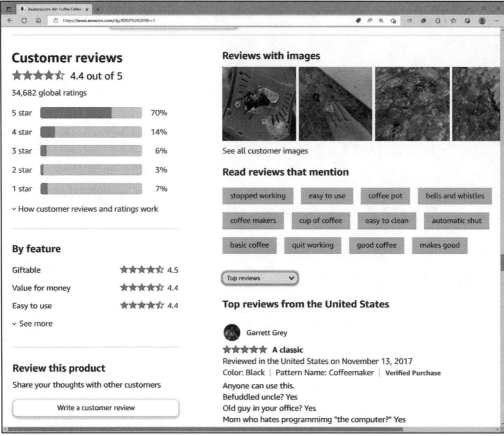

Figure 6.14

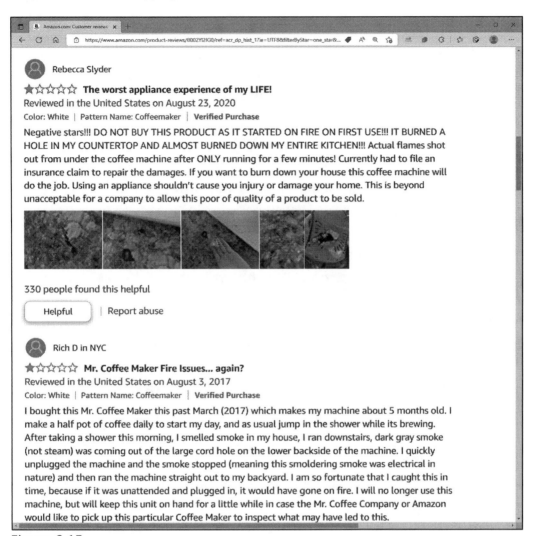

Figure 6.15

So be sure to read reviews when shopping online for things, especially if they are costly items, to see what other people think. If you are buying something you have bought before and know you like it, then you can pretty much ignore what others have to say. Just try not to make your decision based solely on what other people think because you might miss out on a great product that would have worked out just fine for you.

Making Secure and Safe Purchases

When buying products online, you want to have the safest experience possible, so you don't end up getting ripped off or have your personal information stolen etc. I will be going over online safety in Chapter 8, but for now I just wanted to go over some key concepts when it comes to staying secure when paying for your purchases.

The most important thing to consider when shopping online is to make sure you are shopping on a safe and reputable site to begin with. If the site looks like it was designed by a child and has spelling and grammar errors, then it might be something you want to stay away from. Or, if it's based out of another country that might not be known for its security, then that's another red flag.

One of the most important things to check for when shopping online is that you are on the site you are supposed to be on and that it's a secure website. Anyone can make a website that looks just like amazon.com, but if the address bar doesn't say amazon.com, then you know something is wrong. You also want to make sure that there is an **S** at the beginning of the address where it says http**s**. If it just says http, then it's not a secure website and you shouldn't be shopping there. Figure 6.15 shows that I am on the amazon.com website and that it's a secure site so I can feel more comfortable giving my credit card information to them.

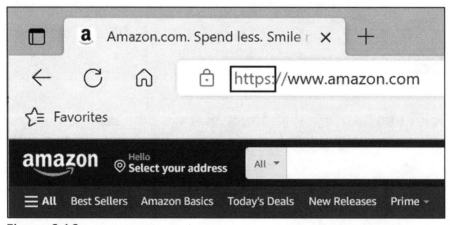

Figure 6.16

Speaking of credit cards, many sites offer you the opportunity to save your shipping and credit card information on the site, so you don't need to type in each time you want to buy something. If it's a site you will be using often, then you might want to save your information, but if it's going to be a one-time thing, then I would advise against it. I also wouldn't save debit card information on a site in case your debit card doesn't have the same type of fraud protection that most credit cards have.

Chapter 7 – Social Media

Social media has been a growing part of the online experience for many years now, and if you haven't gotten on the bandwagon, you are missing out (well, that depends on who you talk to!). There are so many social media sites and apps now that it's impossible to cover them all (since some of them disappear as fast as they show up), so I will go over the most popular sites in this chapter.

For the most part, social media is a good way to connect with friends and family that you aren't able to see on a regular basis. It's also a great way to promote something like a business or charity to get more people aware that they exist. (Of course, you also have the people who abuse these sites by promoting illegal and immoral things or by trying to scam others out of money etc.).

Facebook

One of the most popular social media sites in the world is Facebook, which has been around since 2004. From what I've heard from the younger generation, it's not "what the kids are into" these days, but it's still very popular among the "older" generations. There is a lot that you can do on Facebook, but I will just go over the most common features to get you up and running so you can decide if you want to be a member or not.

Facebook is a way for you to post stories, pictures, movies, website links, and so on for things that you are interested in or are involved in. Many people use it to do things like post pictures of their pets or vacations or complain about their co-workers etc., while others use it to make their followers aware of a certain cause that they are passionate about.

When I say followers, what I mean is the people that are following them on the Facebook site. You can't just follow anyone you want but have to do what is called a friend request, which has to be accepted by the person you have sent the request to. So, if you did a search for Joe Smith and find the Joe Smith you are looking for, you can send him a friend request. Then Joe can either accept or reject that request. If he accepts it, then you will be able to see what Joe is posting on his Facebook page and interact with his posts by doing things such as giving him "likes" and making comments on his posts.

Facebook uses what they call a timeline on your main page that shows you posts from people that you are friends with, and also other people or groups that you follow. For example, if you like the band The Rolling Stones, you can find their Facebook page and then click on *Follow*. You will then be following them and will see their posts in your timeline. For pages like this, you don't need to be accepted in order to see their posts because they are public pages that people (including you) can create in order to get exposure from others. Figure 7.1 shows what I get when searching for The Rolling Stones. You can sort your searches by things such as people, photos, pages and so on.

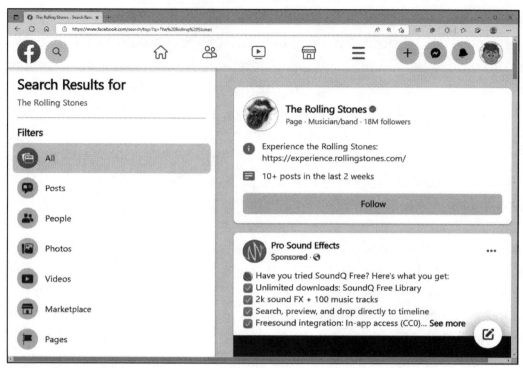

Figure 7.1

Figure 7.2 shows a sample Facebook home page, and, as you can see, there is a lot going on here, so it's easy to get overwhelmed if you are new to the site. But just because it's there doesn't mean you need to use it. If you just want to use Facebook to keep in touch with friends, then it's pretty easy to use and you can then ignore all the other features if you don't think you will want to use them.

The left hand column shows you all the types of areas that you can go to within Facebook such as finding friends, playing games, checking out movies, and so on. The right side of the page shows which of your friends are either online or have been online recently. If there is a green dot next to their name, then that means they are currently online (either on their computer or mobile device), and you can send them an instant message if you want to start up a conversation. Instant messages work sort of like the text messages on your phone.

Figure 7.2

The middle of the page shows your feed, which will consist of posts from your friends and also other pages you follow (such as the one in my Rolling Stones example). It will also display advertisements, so don't get confused if something shows up you don't recognize. You will also see things like suggested groups, friend requests, and so on.

At the top of the page there is a Create Post section where you can post anything that is on your mind and also attach things like photos, videos, your location, and so on. You can also decide where you want your post to show and who can see it.

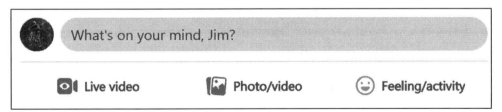

Figure 7.3

Also at the top left of the page is a link with your name and profile picture on it (if you added one). Clicking on that will show you the posts you have recently made as well as other things such as your bio, friend information, likes, etc.

If something looks different than what you see here, it's most likely because Facebook and other websites often change things around which forces us to figure out what they did so we can continue with what we were doing!

Instagram

If you are into sharing pictures of things like your pets, vacations, friends, or just about anything else, then Instagram is for you, since that's pretty much what Instagram is used for. You can view your and others' Instagram accounts on your computer on a mobile device such as your smartphone or tablet even though it's really meant to be used on your phone.

When you create an Instagram account you are the only one who will see your posts until you start acquiring followers, and then they will see your posts every time you upload a picture to your feed. So, if you make an account and want others to follow you, then you will need to notify them and tell them to look up your account name on Instagram to start following you.

You can follow others as well, and they don't even need to be people you know. Many people (such as celebrities or athletes) make their accounts public so anyone can follow them. If you don't want your account to be seen by anyone except people you want to see it, then you can make it private. Business accounts won't have this option, but you will most likely be using a personal account anyway. Once you make your account private, people will have to send you a follow request to see your posts, your followers list, or your following list.

Figure 7.4 shows an example of a post from my mountain bike Instagram account when looking at it on a smartphone. It shows how many likes that particular post got, as well as any comments that my followers have left about that post.

Figure 7.4

Followers can click on the heart icon to like the post or click on the speech bubble icon to leave a comment. They can also share my posts with other people via things like email or text message etc.

Figure 7.5 shows how my account looks on a web browser when using a personal computer. Notice how you can still do the same things such as like and comment on posts and you can click the + button to add a photo from your computer to create a new post.

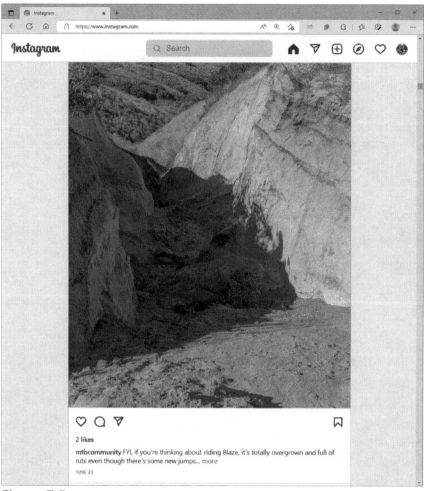

Figure 7.5

To create an account all you need to do is install the Instagram app on your device if it's not there already. Or you can go to the Instagram website on your computer to create an account. Then sign up with a username, email address, and password. Since there are so many Instagram accounts already active, it might take you a bit to find a name that is not already in use.

Then all you need to do is click on the **+** button (which can be seen at the bottom of figure 7.4) and you will be asked where you want to get your photo (or video) from that you wish to post. You can choose from pictures you already have on your device, or you can take one on the spot to post.

Next, you will have the option to enhance your picture with a filter to change the way it looks (figure 7.6).

Figure 7.6

Then you can add some text describing the picture. In my example, I added Fun times on the mountain. Then you can add what they call a tag to your post. Tags are used to reference other people, companies, products, websites, and so on. You create a tag by adding the pound or hash sign (#) to the front of the word you are using for your tag. These are also referred to as hashtags. As you start typing in your hashtag (starting with the # symbol), Instagram will give you suggestions based on what you are typing. You can choose the one that matches or add your own if they don't have a suggestion for you (figure 7.7). If you are just using Instagram for a personal account, you will most likely not have a need for hashtags and can just leave them out of your posts.

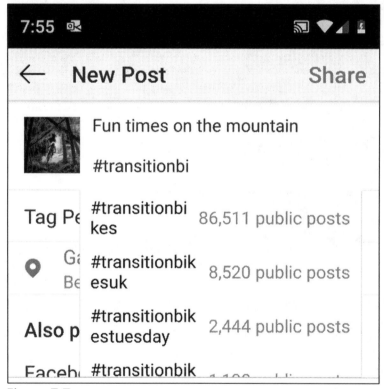

Figure 7.7

Once everything looks good, you will click on *Share*, and then your picture will be posted and show up in all of your follower's feeds on their accounts.

Twitter

Twitter is similar to Instagram except it's used more for posting comments or opinions rather than pictures (even though you can add those as well). You can use your mobile devices and computer to post to your Twitter account, as well as read other people's posts (which are called Tweets).

Just like with Facebook and Instagram, all you need to do is sign up for a free account and you will be ready to start posing. But, once again, you will need to get yourself some followers if you want anyone to read about what you have to say.

Figure 7.8 shows my computer support site Twitter account. On the top you can see that I have made 1,221 tweets to my 220 followers. Then you can see my latest post was a YouTube video on how to export your Instagram data to your computer.

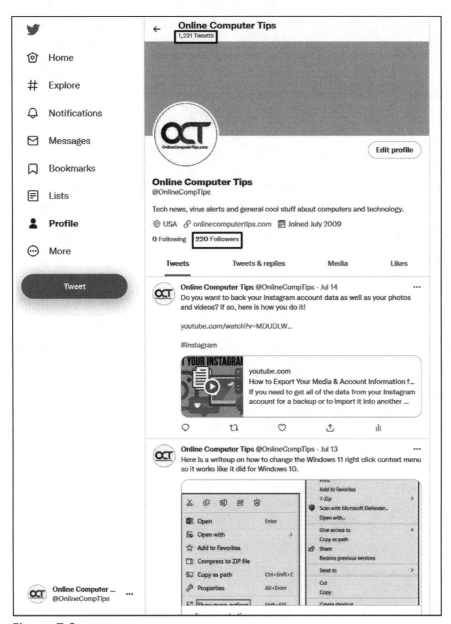

Figure 7.8

To create a new post, all I need to do is click on the *Tweet* button on the left side of the page and fill in the details about my tweet (figure 7.9). In my example, I am going to share a YouTube video about how to remove images from a Word document. I could also click the add image button at the lower left to add a picture to my post, but Twitter will actually show a thumbnail image of the YouTube video from my link so that's good enough for my purposes.

As of now, you can have a maximum of 280 characters per post. (By characters I mean letters, numbers, special characters, and so on.) When you add a website address like I did, it will count towards the character limit.

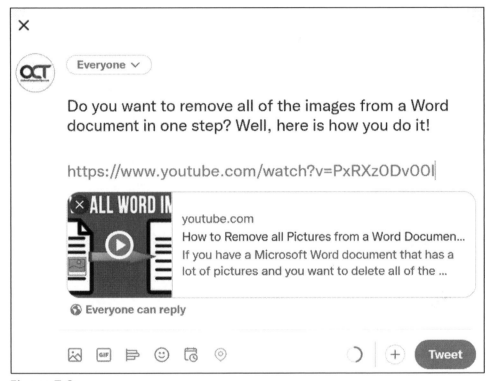

Figure 7.9

You can add other items such as a poll, location, and even emoji characters. When you are ready to add your witty and profound comment, simply click on the *Tweet* button and it will be posted to your account and your followers will see it as well. Figure 7.10 shows my account after adding my new Tweet which is shown above my previous Tweet.

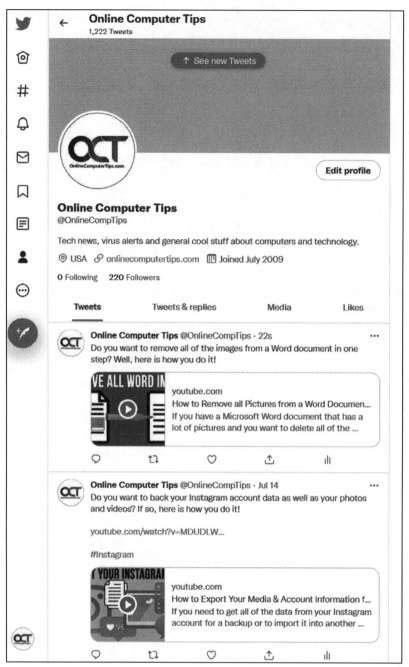

Figure 7.10

Chapter 8 – Staying Safe and Secure Online

If you are new to the Internet, or just not a very tech-savvy person, then this will be one of the most important chapters for you to focus on because the Internet can be a dangerous place and it seems to be getting worse and worse every year. There are many websites out there that will try and get you to give them your personal information, buy services you will never get, or ones that will even install software on your computer to take advantage of you without you even knowing it. Plus, you still need to worry about these types of things happening with the email that you most likely get on a regular basis.

Common Types of Online Threats

There are many ways for people to get to you online, and in this section, I will go over the most commonly used methods these "cybercriminals", as they are often called, use to commit their crimes.

The first one I want to discuss is what is known as a drive by attack or drive by download. This is when you go to a website and some type of software or file gets downloaded to your computer that is used to do things such as steal your personal information or cause unwanted popup ads, etc. This term can also be used when you purposely download software from a website thinking it's one thing, but it turns out to be something malicious.

Unfortunately, many of these sites are good at tricking those who are too trusting or may not know any better, and once you go to that site it's too late and then you will need to find a way to clean this "malware infection", as it is called, from your computer. Many times this software is very good at keeping itself hidden so you don't even know it's there. I will be discussing security software later in this chapter, but many of these products can actually tell when this process is happening and block it or prevent you from going to the malicious site at all.

What you can do on your end is not go to any type of website that you don't think is legitimate. Many times people will get this type of malware (or spyware as it's also called) infection when looking for things like free music or movie downloads. These cybercriminals will prey on those looking to get something for free that would normally not be free. Pornography sites are also notorious for spreading malware so stay off those as well.

Another scam you may come across is getting a message on your computer saying that you have some type of virus or spyware infection, and you need to call a certain number to get it fixed otherwise your computer will stop working and you may even lose your personal files. Many times these messages will say they are from Microsoft trying to legitimize themselves. Then once you call the number, they will ask for your credit card first, and then have you help them get on your computer remotely so they can "fix" the problem that was not even there to begin with. Figure 8.1 shows an example of what this message can look like, but they can vary dramatically in their appearance.

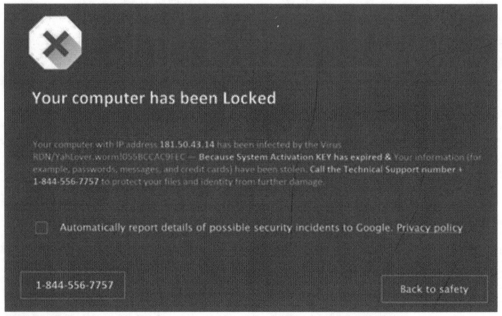

Figure 8.1

Many times they will often install malware on your computer while pretending to fix it, so it's a double whammy because you lost money and also made your computer worse off than it was before. Just remember that Microsoft, Apple, Dell, HP, and so on will never call you to tell you that your computer has malicious software installed on it (they have better things to do!).

If this happens to you, just try and close out the message and your web browser, and if that doesn't work then shut down your computer. If you are prevented from that, then you will need to hold down the power button to force the power off or pull the plug from the wall and hope everything works correctly after you turn your computer back on.

 It's never a good idea to simply turn off your computer without properly shutting it down because you risk file corruption and data loss that may make your computer not want to start back up again.

Another common way for cybercriminals to get your personal information is to create fake websites that copy legitimate websites in order to trick you into giving up your personal information such as passwords, credit card numbers, social security numbers, and so on.

They do this by duplicating an existing website, and many of them look so much like the real website that it's hard to tell the difference unless you know what you are looking for. Some things that will give away the fraudulent sites are spelling and grammar errors as well as low quality graphics and odd looking text.

The way to distinguish the real site from the fake site is by its URL, or address as most people refer to it. Many times these sites will have a similar address, but just be off by one letter hoping you won't be looking or notice the difference. For example, if your banking site address is **http://www.safebank.com**, then a fake version might have an address of **http://saferbank.com** and count on you not noticing the difference. Then they would send you a fake email with a link to the fake site saying something like there is a problem with your account and hope that you go there and log in, which will give them your name and password to the real site that they can use for their own evil purposes. Thankfully you can't have two websites with the exact same address, otherwise we would all be in a lot of trouble!

There are other types of online threats you should be aware of as well, and I will be covering more of them in detail in the following sections.

Secure vs. Unsecure Websites

By now you should have realized that the Internet is not a 100% safe place to be and that there are risks involved when going online. Thankfully there are some methods that are used to help keep you safe when surfing the Internet. One of these methods involves securing websites in order to assure you that you are going to the site you want to be going to. This might be more than you need or want to know but to make a website secure, the administrator needs to purchase a certificate from a trusted certificate authority and install it on the website to prove that they are who they say they are, and that all information passed back and forth between your computer or device and the website is over a secure connection. Most modern web browsers will let you know when your connection is secure or unsecure, but still let you access the site either way.

Just because a website is not secure doesn't mean that it can't be trusted and that you should avoid going to it. Many websites don't have any need to be secured because they are just for informational purposes and there is no need for you to input any personal information while on that site.

You might have noticed that website addresses begin with **http** even though many browsers hide the http and even the www in the address bar. When a site begins with http, that means it's not secure, and your browser should display a warning like the one seen in figure 8.2 (which is actually my mountain bike website). As you can see, it just shows www.mtbcommunity.com and doesn't even show the entire address with the http in front of it which would look like **http://www.mtbcommunity.com**.

Figure 8.2

On my computer website I do have a certificate installed, and many websites are going with certificates even if they really don't need them just so they can assure you of their security. Notice in figure 8.3 that the address begins with https, and the **S** at the end stands for secure. There is also a lock icon next to the address indicating that it's a secure website.

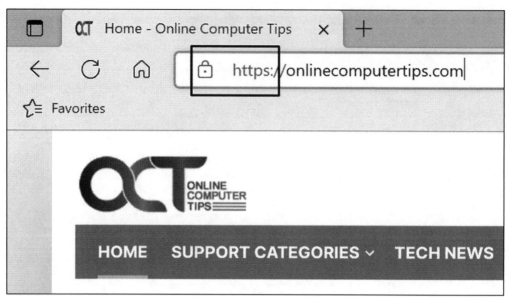

Figure 8.3

If you are going to a website where you will be logging in with a username and password or entering any kind of personal information into a form, then you need to make sure that it is a secure website, otherwise you risk getting your information stolen. If it's a banking website or shopping website, then you really need to make sure that it is secure otherwise you are asking for trouble. Any banking or shopping website that is not secure should not be up and running and might even be a fake site to begin with.

Email Safety
If you are an active Internet user, then you most likely have an email account as well that you use for personal or business emails. I'm sure from time to time (or daily) you have received emails from people that you don't know or about subjects that don't concern you at all.

Just like they do with websites, cybercriminals will try and get to you via your email as well, so always be careful when opening any email you get, even if it's from someone you know. There are many ways these individuals will try and trick you in order to get your personal data or infect your computer with some sort of malware.

Spoofed Emails

The first email safety topic I want to discuss involves spoofing emails with names and addresses you know in order to trick you into thinking it's from someone you trust when, in fact, it's not. Spoofing an email involves either putting in the name of someone you know as the sender, or having their real email address displayed, or maybe even both.

When you create an email account, you can put in whatever name you like for the display name, which is what is shown to the person you send an email to. So, if someone knows the name of someone you trust, then it's easy to just put that name as their display name and hope you don't check the email address to make sure it's really them.

It's also possible for an actual email address to be spoofed so it looks like it's really coming from that person. If you are not careful, then you can be tricked by this as well. There are ways to check the real email address of a sender, but that varies depending on what site or program you use to access your email. You might have even received an email from yourself at one time and wondered how that was possible, and that's a perfect example of address spoofing.

Fake Website Links

Another common practice is to add a fake website link in the body of an email hoping you click on it so it will take you to maybe a fake version of that website or another site where it installs some malware on your computer without you knowing it.

It's easy to have the link display text be different from where the website is actually taking you, so you should always confirm where it's going. Most of the time you can hover your mouse over the link and it will tell you the real address of the website (as seen in figure 8.4). if you look closely, you can see that the display text for the link shows **www.safebank.com** while the real website address is actually

www.fakebank.com. This procedure will be harder or not possible on mobile devices, so you should be extra careful.

Figure 8.4

Malicious Attachments

Another thing to watch out for when it comes to email is making sure not to open any attachments that you shouldn't be opening. I know it's hard to tell just by looking at an attachment whether it's safe or not to open, but there are a few things to watch out for to increase your chances of staying safe.

The first rule in opening email attachments is NEVER OPEN AN ATTACHMENT FROM SOMEONE YOU DON'T KNOW. This is a very common practice used by cybercriminals to get their way into your computer.

There are several types of attachments you should never open regardless of who they are from. Even if it's from someone you know, there is a good chance their email account got hacked, or someone is spoofing their email address and sending you a malicious attachment. Files generally have what they call file extensions on them, and these file extensions tell your computer or device what program to use to open the file with. For example, a Microsoft Word document will have a **.doc** or **.docx** file extension on it telling your computer to open a file called **resume.docx** with Microsoft Word.

Many operating systems, such as Windows, will hide these file extensions by default, so the file I just mentioned will show only as resume without the .docx. There is a way to have Windows show the file extensions, but that is beyond the scope of this book, so if you are feeling geeky you can research it yourself and figure out how to get it done (it's not that hard).

Now that I got file extensions out of the way, back to the types of files you shouldn't open. There are many dangerous file types that you would never need to open on your computer or device, so if you see any files that end with any of these, just delete the email and remove it from your trash.

- .js
- .exe
- .bat
- .vbs
- .vb
- .dll
- .jar
- .sfx
- .tmp
- .py
- .pif
- .ps

These are not the only files to watch out for but are some of the more commonly used files that are used to spread malware. Keep in mind that these types of files have legitimate uses on computers, but not as email attachments.

There are other types of files that are commonly sent as attachments that can still be malicious, so you still need to be careful even when opening these types of files.

This is where having security software installed on your computer will help protect you before it's too late by scanning the file before you even get a chance to open it. (I will be discussing this type of software later in the chapter.)

Checking Website Addresses

Earlier in this chapter, I discussed secure and unsecure websites, but I wanted to mention how you should check the website addresses of the sites you go to whenever possible to make sure you are going where you want to go.

If you get to your commonly accessed websites from your bookmarks, then you should be okay because they don't change unless you manually change them. (Just be sure your bookmark addresses are correct to begin with!) But if you do a search for a website such as your banking site, then make sure the link you are clicking on from the search results is the right one.

Figure 8.5 shows the results I get when searching for *Peoples Bank*. As you can see, there are several results, and they all have different addresses, so it's important to know the right address of the site you are trying to go to when it has to do with security, or a site where you might have to enter your personal information.

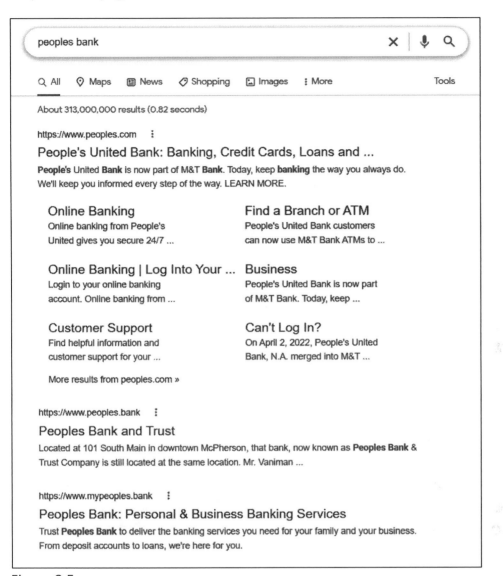

Figure 8.5

If you look closely at all the search results in figure 8.5, you will see that all the addresses start with https, meaning they are secure websites, which is critical for banking sites to be. Try and get in the habit of noticing this in your search results for your own safety.

This also applies when people email or text website addresses to you. Before you click or tap on the link, give it a once over to make sure that everything looks okay so you can have an idea of what website it will be taking you to rather than just blindly clicking and hoping for the best.

Providing Personal Information

When you do things like shop or bank online, you are expected to provide certain types of information such as your address, phone number, account number, and so on. But this doesn't mean you should just give any site the information they ask for. If you are on a site that does not require you to give out any information, then there is really no reason to do so. For example, you might go to a website, and it will give you a popup to sign up for its mailing list. If you don't plan on using this site again or want to get emails from them, then don't feel obligated to provide them with your email address.

Many times you will go to a website such as a shopping site and it will want to know your location to show you their local stores, or maybe estimate shipping costs. When this happens you may get a popup similar to what is shown in figure 8.6.

Figure 8.6

If you are okay with providing the site with your location, then you can click on *Allow* and it will tailor its results based on where you are. For the most part, there is no harm in doing this, but if you really don't have a need to give them your location, you might as well click on *Block*.

When shopping online you will often get asked if you want to save information such as your shipping address or credit card number. This is completely up to you because that way you won't need to type in the information each time you buy something from that site. I'm usually okay with saving my address on sites that I use often, but for the most part, I don't let them keep my credit card information. (I do make one exception for Amazon.com because of how often I use their site).

 You should **never** give out your social security number unless you are sure the site is secure. When typing it in you should see that what you are typing is hidden as you type (******). If it's not, then that might be an indication that you shouldn't be entering it in there.

Saving Your Login Information

Since technology has made our lives easier, it has unfortunately made us lazier as well. Nobody likes to type in their username and password every time they go to a website or have to remember what password they even use for that site. All web browsers offer the ability to remember login information for specific websites so that when you go to that website, the information is already filled in for you or, better yet, it just logs you in automatically.

For many sites this is okay as long as it's a website that won't cause you any personal or financial problems if someone was to get your login information. But for things such as banking, tax, or medical websites, you should never let your web browser save your login information because if someone gets into your computer, they will be able to get your saved names and passwords and will be able to use them to log into things such as your bank accounts, etc.

Figure 8.7 shows some of the saved passwords kept in the Google Chrome web browser. All you need to know to view any of these passwords is the password for the computer itself, so you can see how easy it would be to have all of your usernames and passwords compromised.

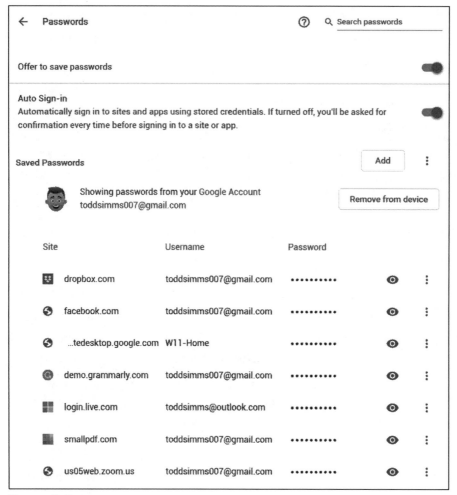

Figure 8.7

If you look closely, you can see the options to turn off the offer to save passwords feature, and also the automatic sign in feature. These settings will vary from browser to browser and device to device.

If you have a saved login that you want to get rid of, you should be able to just remove the saved information for that site rather than have to remove all of them or disable the ability for your web browser to save logins\passwords altogether. (How you do this will vary on your browser and device, of course.)

Clearing Browser History

There may come a time when you want to erase where you have been from your browser while in normal browsing mode. This is where clearing your history comes into play, and it's something you can easily do whenever you like. As you access websites, your computer or mobile device keeps track of where you have been and also does things like keeps images from sites so when you go back to that site it doesn't have to re-download the images from that page and rather just loads the ones on your computer, making that site load faster.

Over time your computer can get cluttered with these images and also other temporary files like cookies that your web browser keeps as you visit websites throughout the day. These files take up space on your hard drive, and over time can even slow things down a little, so clearing your history and temporary files is something you might want to think about doing.

Most browsers will let you choose what type of information and files you can delete and also from what time period. So, let's say you want to remove your browsing history for the past week, but leave the rest. You most likely will have an option to do that. Or let's say you want to delete temporary Internet files but keep your cookies. That should be an option you have as well.

Just like with everything else, how you clear your history will vary depending on what web browser you are using. If you are using the Microsoft Edge browser, you can click on the ellipsis (...) at the upper right corner of the screen and then click on *History* to see your history and history settings.

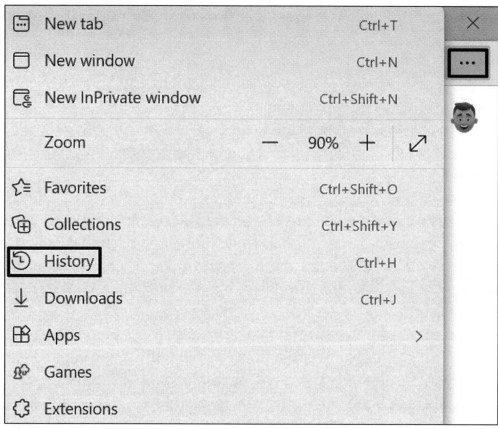

New tab	Ctrl+T
New window	Ctrl+N
New InPrivate window	Ctrl+Shift+N
Zoom	— 90% + ↗
Favorites	Ctrl+Shift+O
Collections	Ctrl+Shift+Y
History	Ctrl+H
Downloads	Ctrl+J
Apps	>
Games	
Extensions	

Figure 8.8

As you can see in figure 8.9, you have the option to clear your browsing data (history), or to open your history page which is shown in figure 8.10.

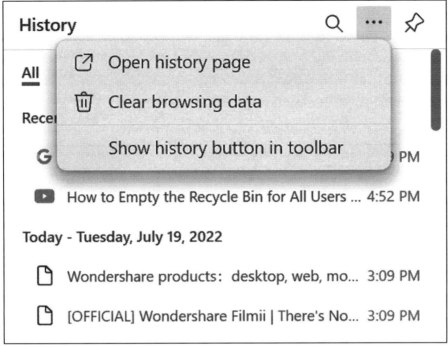

Figure 8.9

From your history page, you can view your browsing history for specific dates or even search your history. You can also clear all of your history or select specific websites from your list and just delete those.

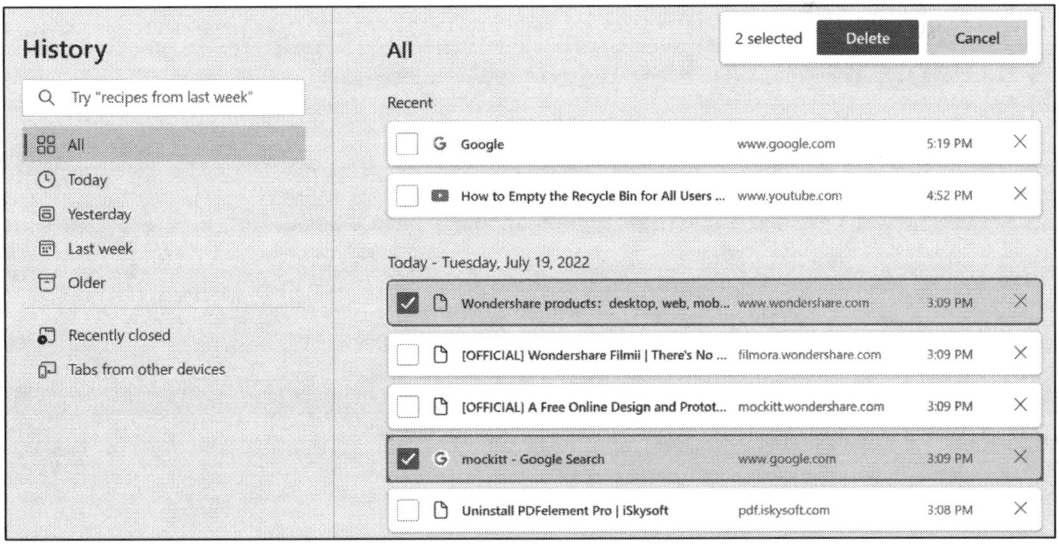

Figure 8.10

Website Popups

These days it's possible to simply go to a website and can end up with unwanted software installed on your computer and not even know it's happened. But if all of a sudden you are getting lots of pop-up ads while browsing the Internet, automatically be taken to other websites or have strange toolbars show up in your browser, then that will confirm that you have been a victim of this type of unwanted software installation.

Popup Ads

Popup ads are exactly what they sound like: ads that pop up out of nowhere on top of whatever webpage you happen to be on. For the most part, you can just close them out, but many times they will just come back over and over and get really annoying. Other times they won't have a way to close them without closing your web browser altogether.

Many websites have legitimate popup ads that might ask you to sign up for their mailing list, ask you to take a survey, offer you a coupon, etc., and this is perfectly normal. Figure 8.11 shows an example of one of these types of popup ads. Usually they will have an X that you can click on to close them or sometimes you can click on a part of the page outside of the ad to make them go away.

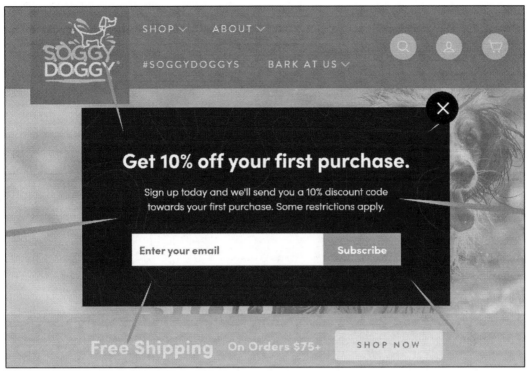

Figure 8.11

When you see popups that are telling you that your computer is infected with a virus or that you need some sort of software update to continue, then it's most likely a popup caused by either malware installed on your computer, or from a website that is trying to get you to install or do something you shouldn't be doing. Figures 8.12 and 8.13 show examples of these types of popups.

Figure 8.12

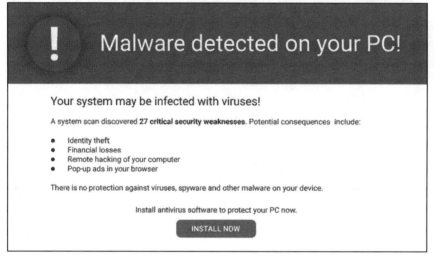

Figure 8.13

The hardest part about dealing with popups is determining which are legitimate and which are caused by malicious software installed on your computer. One way to tell is if you get constant pop-up ads on any website you go to compared to if it's just on a particular site. If it's just on the one site and it doesn't happen when you leave that site and go to another, then it's most likely just the way that website has been designed, and it might be one you want to stay away from. If you get popup ads all the time on any site you go to, then it's probably time to get some antispyware software installed on your computer to see if it can get rid of it.

Online Banking and Bill Paying

One of my favorite things about the Internet is not having to write checks, address envelopes, and buy stamps to pay my bills. And even better, I like how I don't have to get paper bills in the mail that I end up having to shred because I don't need to keep them for any reason. (Plus, all the unnecessary tree killing!) It's also nice to be able to check your credit card balance and purchases any time you want.

Thanks to online banking and bill paying, it's much easier to stay organized and make sure all your bills are paid on time. The only downside is having to risk exposing your information such as account numbers, your social security number, usernames, and passwords online since it's all going over the Internet to a server who knows where. But if you use caution (and common sense), you will be just fine. Plus, most banks and credit cards offer protection against online theft and fraud.

Once you have an account with your bank or utility company, it's very easy to sign up for an online account. Simply go to their website and enter your information to prove it's you. This information might be in the form of an account number, credit card number, name, address, and so on. (Just make sure you are on the official site for that company before giving out any of this information!)

Then once you have your account configured, you simply sign in with the username and password you created, and you are good to go. (Many times your username will be your email address.)

It's a good idea to provide your phone number when signing up for an online account because it can be used to verify it's really you when logging in from a new device, or if you need to reset your password in case you forget it.

Figure 8.14 shows a typical credit card site where you can see things such as the balance owed, credit limit, payment information, payment due date, recent transactions, and more. All of this information is at your fingertips any time you need it, and if you want to see something like an older statement, all you need to do is choose an older date.

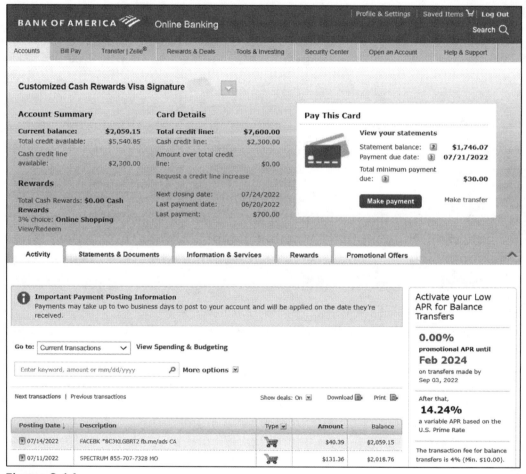

Figure 8.14

To make a payment in this example, you would just click the *Make Payment* button, put in the amount you wish to pay and the date you wish to pay it, and they will take care of the rest. You will need to first set up a payment method such as your checking account beforehand in order for them to have a place to take the money from.

Like I've said many times thought out this book, what you see in my examples will not always look exactly like what you will see when you try this yourself because each website is different, plus the web browser and device you use will make a difference as well.

Downloading Files and Software

Downloading files and software to install on your computer might not be something you ever do but I wanted to take the time to discuss what can happen if you download the wrong types of files and software.

You should know by now that the Internet can be a dangerous place, and there are some shady characters out there looking to take advantage of you, so you really need to be careful when it comes to watching what you download online. If you keep your downloading limited to well known, trusted websites, then you should be okay.

For the most part, files like pictures and music should be okay because you can't really do anything to make these types of files dangerous. But let's say you are looking for an instruction manual for your new iPad. This type of document will most likely be in a PDF file format, which is very common and usually safe. But it's possible to create a PDF file that can infect your computer when it's opened. So, if you go to the official Apple website to get this manual, you should be safe, but if you see it listed on a website that doesn't appear too professional or trustworthy, you might want to think twice about downloading it from there. Over time it gets a little easier to tell the good from the bad websites, but it can still be difficult if you are not a techy-type person.

Many sites offer documentation in Microsoft Word format as well, which is also generally safe, but you need to be careful when downloading Word files, too. The same thing goes for zip files, which are also very common. I mentioned potentially dangerous email attachments earlier in this chapter, and those same types of files apply when it comes to downloading files from the Internet.

One thing that you can download that is potentially more dangerous than files is software. In order to install new software on your computer, you need a way to get it there first. This can be done via methods such as CDs, flash drives, and downloading it directly from the Internet.

When downloading software from the Internet, where you get it from can make all the difference in the world. Let's say you wanted to buy a copy of Microsoft Office to install on your home computer. You can find this software in many places, such as the Microsoft site or on Amazon, etc. If you purchase and download Office from one of these reputable sites, then you will most likely be okay. If you were to download Office from somewhere that might not seem so legitimate, you never know what you might end up with. It might be the wrong version, not come with an installation serial number\key, or may not even be Office at all! This might seem a little over-exaggerated, which it is, but I just want to point out that you shouldn't just download software from anywhere that is convenient or says they have the best deal.

Free Software
When it comes to downloading software, the ones that don't cost you anything are the ones to watch out for. The same thing applies here as it does with retail software. You need to consider where you are getting the software from before downloading it.

Many software providers will hide malicious software inside of their programs as a way to infect your computer without you knowing it. And by installing this software, you are the one who has actually infected your own computer! Sometimes when installing software you will get prompted to install additional software at the same time, and this is where they can get you as well if you are not paying attention. So if you ever see this happen, just say no and it might be a sign that the software you downloaded might not be something you want to install either.

Figure 8.15 shows an example of legitimate software wanting to install additional software, which I always say no to as well because, for the most part, you don't want or need this extra software. If you are not paying attention and are just clicking Next through the screens, you might not see the checkbox and unintentionally install the extra software and then have to go and remove it later on.

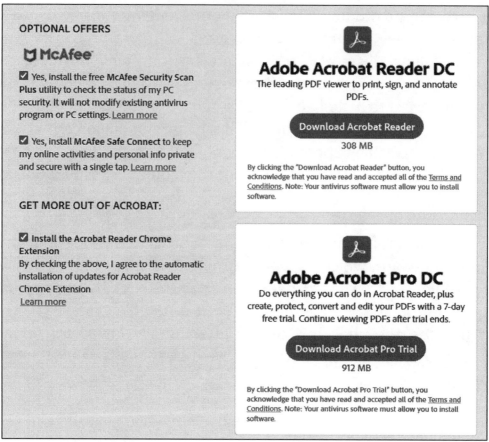

Figure 8.15

Security Software

Now that I have most likely made you afraid to use the Internet, it's time to discuss some of the software out there that you can use to protect yourself from those who are out to get you. There are many options when it comes to this type of software, and some are free while others will cost you a little money. And believe it or not, there is also software out there that is designed to look like it's meant to protect you when, in fact, it's really only going to cause your computer harm.

You might have heard the terms "antivirus software" and also "antispyware" or "antimalware software" and are wondering what the difference is. Viruses, spyware, and malware all fall under the same category, spyware and malware basically being two different words for the same thing.

Viruses are designed to harm your computer and spread to other computers over networks and things such as shared USB drives. Spyware, on the other hand, is designed to steal information from you or find a way to make money off of you. You will find that spyware is more of an issue lately than viruses just because cybercriminals are more concerned with making money compared to breaking computers. With that being said, it's still necessary to have protection from both viruses and spyware\malware.

When it comes to antivirus software, there are many options out there to choose from with some being free and others costing money. I have found that the free ones actually do a good job, and there is not really a need to pay for the software. You might have to deal with some advertisements popping up or the software telling you that you can get advanced features with the pay-for version, but it's really not much of a hassle. If you are running Windows on your computer, then it will most likely come with built-in virus protection (depending on what version of Windows you are running). Macs don't really have a problem with viruses mainly because there are so many computers running Windows compared to Mac OS that hackers devote their time to Windows. You will hear people say that Macs are more secure, but they are susceptible to viruses as well. There just aren't as many out there.

Some of the free antivirus software that I have tried and like include the following.

- Sophos Home Antivirus
- AVG Free Antivirus
- Avast Free Antivirus
- Avira Free Antivirus

As for antispyware software, you also have many options of which some are free and some you have to pay for. Once again, there are some free options that work quite well. When shopping for antispyware software, make sure you do your research and read real reviews so you don't end up installing the type that will actually cause more harm than good. Antivirus software generally runs in the background at all times and monitors everything you do, while antispyware software usually needs to be run manually to scan for issues. There are some products out there that will also monitor for spyware in real time. Here are a few antispyware products that I can recommend:

- Malwarebytes (They have a free version as well as a pay-for version that monitors in real time.)
- Spybot Search & Destroy 2 Anti Spyware
- Comodo Cleaning Essentials Security\Spyware Scanner
- Malwarebytes AdwCleaner Scanner

These types of products are also available for mobile devices but are not needed as much as they are on computers (especially Windows), and you can get similar types of apps for free. Once again, just be sure you are not installing something that will end up causing you problems rather than fixing problems.

 When downloading apps for your mobile device, be sure to check how many times the app has been downloaded. If it has thousands or hundreds of thousands of downloads, then there is a better chance it is legitimate compared to one that only has a few hundred downloads.

With a little caution and a lot of common sense, you can keep yourself pretty safe online and have fun discovering what the Internet has to offer. Just make sure you don't spend too much time online and not get anything else done!